The Art and Skill
of
Ingenious Selling

The Art and Skill
of
Ingenious Selling

by

George B. Wright

Parker Publishing Company, Inc.   West Nyack, N.Y.

This book is dedicated to Carl E. Priest, a veteran of forty-six years in sales for The Parker Pen Company, now Senior Vice-President and Member of the Board of Directors, to whom I owe gratitude for many valuable techniques used in mastering the art and skill of ingenious selling.

About the Author

Following a self-earned, "depression era" college degree, George Wright joined the Parker Pen Company as a sales correspondent and field sales trainee. Now, as National Sales Manager, his experience spans thirty years as Salesman, District Manager for thirteen states in the south, Manager of the Midwestern Division and National Wholesale Sales Manager. He has interviewed and sold thousands of retailers and wholesalers, both alone and in the company of at least two hundred salesmen. He has been a trainer, counselor, disciplinarian, and friend to salesmen all of his working life. His experience includes grass-roots selling and sophisticated marketing. He is at home in a neighborhood drug store or plush salon, at ease with a working buyer or the president of a multi-million-dollar corporation.

The writing instrument business embraces the drug field, the stationery and equipment industry, the department store and jewelry businesses, as well as others. Mr. Wright has a wide acquaintanceship throughout all of these trade classification areas and a deep understanding of both the retail and wholesale operations within them. He has also participated in trade association, marketing, and training sessions in these fields and has intimate knowledge of the varied sales and marketing problems involved. He characterizes himself as a problem solver.

George Wright is a graduate of the University of Wisconsin and Madison Business College. He served as a U. S. Navy Lieutenant aboard ship in the Pacific Area during World War II. As National Sales Manager of his company, he is an active member of trade, sales, and marketing organizations within his industry. He has published industry articles and has participated in and conducted literally hundreds of sales meetings and conferences.

Mr. Wright's self-development techniques have been proved by millions of dollars in sales gained through their application by successful writing industry salesmen. His first book explores a new approach to selling success developed through his years of rich sales and marketing experience.

The Art and Skill of
Ingenious Selling

The Factors That Caused Me to Write This Book....

This book, written for the professional salesman and sales manager, describes a different and more productive way to sell. Its principles can be adapted to the whole spectrum of the field of selling. It is a book designed to provide strong assistance for the man who has decided upon sales, merchandising and marketing as a career; it will aid him in attaining his immediate personal sales goals and in realizing his future ambitions.

It may seem mystifying that so many salesmen who are naturally interesting and stimulating in their everyday lives are lackluster and boring in their professional lives. These salesmen have, by design, tried to make themselves what they are not. They seem to feel the job of selling is one that requires a changed approach from the job of living. If there is any profession that requires naturalness and the projection of one's own personality, it is in the field of selling. This book will highlight ways to employ and improve natural talents to get results—in *any* field of selling.

Much has been and is being written today about the evolution of modern marketing and markets and the effect upon the salesman and his future. The multiple store Buying Committee is an example in point.

Apparently, some experts have written personal selling off as useless and dying because a few mass marketers have chosen the buying committee as the decision-making factor in the selection of their retail lines. The buying committee plan allows the salesman only a few minutes before a buyer. He makes a succinct outline of his proposition, and the buyer then takes it to the buying committee, which acts upon it objectively. The salesman supposedly has no opportunity to inject emotionalism or personality into his sales presentation and thereby affect the sales decision. He doesn't even have an opportunity to follow the age-old formula for making the sale: get interest, make the presentation, close effectively.

Yet, the facts are that the salesman *can* be (and already is) a tremendous factor in the buying committee method of product selection. It all depends upon the salesman. We will discuss proved techniques for swinging these "absentee" sales.

Today, more and more, the computer is being touted as an "inventory to order" retail plan for eliminating the buying function. In other words, all the buyer of the store has to do is to punch in his inventory (or his computer maintains a perpetual inventory), relay this information on to the supplier, and the supplier's computer figures out the order from an inventory control standpoint. The salesman is "eliminated"—the buyer is "eliminated." All that is necessary is a key punch operator.

The computer will indeed become an increasingly powerful force in American business, but in the foreseeable future the computer is going to have little impact on retail/wholesale buying for the successful merchant. New products and new marketing ideas are too important a factor in success at the point of sale to make the computer practical at this juncture. Yet, there is a movement to mechanize on standard items, and we will explore the salesman's role in this development.

These are but two specific examples of changed market conditions today. There are many more. Our mobile and growing population, our mass communications systems, the welfare state concept of the Great Society, the new affluence of our people, are broader aspects of changing patterns that greatly affect selling direction.

Yet, however changed this market pattern is today, much of sales training is still hammered out in the same old stereotyped fashion. Anyone who has gone through the gauntlet of "how to get into the big leagues in selling" will recognize that most efforts to define selling and explain the selling function seem to reduce it to a step-by-step formula. All the successful salesman need do is "have a good memory and follow the book."

Really, selling is the most human of all professions. It is a natural phenomenon, actually more a trait or a characteristic than a profession. Selling is an absolute necessity in the business relationship, but it is the very essence of the human relationship. This book, however, is *not* a psychological analysis of selling. It will debunk the formula method and establish a new and very different approach for self-improvement in the selling field.

There is much speculation about so-called creative selling. A better description is *ingenious selling*. While a salesman with average intelligence can learn ways to apply himself in a "creative" manner, it is simpler and more effective to develop sales *skills* of an "ingenious" nature. To do this, we can adapt a learning process similar to that of the actor who improves his acting skills with the so-called *method acting* system.

In the selling function, as it applies to today's problems, there really is no basic formula, i.e., a set sales pattern from introduction to close. There are easy, natural guideposts which are recognized immediately, but not stereotyped guideposts which must be dutifully remembered and which only tend to confuse the salesman along the path to a successful sale. The salesman will naturally fall into enough routines and habit patterns, some of them bad ones, without consciously trying to develop them.

Certainly, there are skills to be learned in selling, skills that are at first very human skills, such as listening and talking with a purpose, which we will define as directed conversation. This is the sales interview. Another human skill which we will call perception is used in such ways as knowing the time to act in a given situation, or simply judging a buyer's reaction. Fortunately, we can learn and develop most of these skills by simply being aware of them and living them day to day—if we know how.

The selling profession can be as gratifying a human endeavor as medicine, law, or the ministry. A simple thing like helping a retailer to do a better product-explaining job to his customers actually helps everyone along the economic line. Considered in its richest sense, a *great* many people are benefited as the result of a successful sale.

Our concern here, however, is not another attempt to elevate the selling profession, but rather to apply, via new techniques, those practical principles of good selling (of which the salesman's attitude is among the most important) and raise the level of individual performance. There is greater opportunity in the field of selling today than ever in the history of our country, and there is a real dearth of good sales talent. The alert, professional salesman is obviously making a serious mistake if he does not learn how to take advantage of this unique situation. The Council of Opportunities in Selling, Incorporated, a non-profit educational organization, traced the backgrounds of presidents of corporations with sales exceeding $500,000,000 yearly. The largest group among the presidents, 27 per cent had started as salesmen.

The only reason that percentage is not even higher is because there just is not enough good sales talent in these corporations to elevate salesmen to these top-level jobs. Make no mistake about it, however, the organization you now work for is right at this moment trying to fill responsible jobs with people of selling-oriented ability. Today's economics of over-abundance dictates that good selling is an absolute requirement for good management.

Let's precisely determine how we can get there, and how we can make it a fruitful and satisfying experience along the way.

Table of Contents

How do you establish specific and detailed long and short range growth objectives for greater day-to-day effectiveness? What are the two basic elements that point the way to increased personal selling efficiency? Examples are shown illustrating how to apply good planning to everyday call-to-call success. How do you use good personal organization as a problem-solving device resulting in increased sales? How do you use your own knowledge and experience more efficiently? How do you inventory and analyze your current job responsibilities with a "job writeup" to exploit as a tool to greater daily results?

To realize full potential, a salesman must work from an infallible record system. Why and how do personal and company records clash? Here is a step-by-step illustrated method to build a useful, meaningful, easy to keep record system that assures selling increases. How to use records to make selling interviews more productive. How to use records for an easy to administer, easy to follow, automatic routing procedure. How to plan a "business guaranteed" routing everytime.

A concise new method to assess your present adeptness in the face-to-face selling interview. A way to measure your skill at using words and language in selling effectiveness. What is the sales "art of directed conversation" and how is it applied? How skilled at persuasion are you? Illustrated examples determine how much more the things you do influence the sale as compared to the things you have, such as advertising, program and products.

This chapter devotes itself exclusively to an analysis of each of the procedures in the successful sale with a view to turning the unexpected event, which oftentimes kills the sale, into an advantage that actually furthers the sale. It carries through detailed explanations and descriptions with examples of: How to Approach the Selling Situation. How to Introduce the Sale. How to Make the Selling Presentation. How to Get the Order. How to Follow Up on the Sale. All of these new selling approaches are catalogued into making the most of each selling opportunity using new and unique methods.

How do you get the ideas that make your whole selling effort more productive? How do you most effectively use these ideas to solve common sales problems for greater results? This chapter describes how you size up buying situations and buyers accurately and how you best handle your sales effort with various buyer types. Examples are explained in connection with angry buyer situations, silent and talkative buyers, new buyers and many others with buyer traits and characteristics outlined. How do you discover the "decision maker" in a selling situation? How to successfully sell the Chain Store. How to organize the big, unwieldy merchandising program. What is "Umbrella Selling"? How to organize and use visual aids more successfully. What really is the "price problem" and what is its most effective solution?

Many salesmen who can sell themselves to their customers successfully fail to really sell themselves to their

Contents

employers. This chapter deals with solving the problems of communication between field sales and management on the subject of personal and financial growth. Why are successful salesmen prime candidates for advancement who most often never progress? How can you reverse that possibility for yourself? How to turn an unrealistic attitude into a realistic opportunity. What are the broad aspects of exploiting outstanding selling results into a successful selling career? A four step plan of procedure is described for making the most of your growth possibilities.

1

The "Opportunity Explosion" in Individual Selling— The Basis for This Book

The biggest boom in the history of the United States keeps right on rolling along, as does "Old Man River," month after month, year after year. There are dips and spurts, peaks and valleys, but the trend is always up, up, up, up. The affluent American is the envy of the world, and our so-called lower and middle classes are rich by any standards of twenty years ago.

This great economic upheaval created by American ingenuity has brought with it vast new horizons in cultural pursuits, scientific advancements, leisure living—and guilty consciences. The bins may just be too overflowing. Many of us, it seems, are afraid to take advantage of prosperity, thinking perhaps that if we ignore it long enough it will go away. Nevertheless, the trend is up, and the Great Society grows richer.

Economists chart it, marketers plan it, and salesmen at all levels often reject it. Salesmen must frequently, therefore, have the sharpest conscience pangs, because they have the greatest opportunity to capitalize on the situation. However, they will never realize anything like their real opportunity unless and until they abandon many of their obsolete work patterns and concepts, and change much of their thinking and doing.

For the alert salesman, both in the near and long term, the financial opportunity represented by this mighty flow of wealth is actually far greater than he has any conception of. His opportunity is more than likely to reside right with the organization or company with whom he is now associated, although it is possible that he might have to make a change to realize it. Naturally, opportunity is greatest for the potentially ingenious salesman who learns to apply new methods to improve his selling skills.

This is the basis for our search to uncover the specifics of "Ingenious Selling." At first, we will examine the reasons why most of the traditional procedures, techniques, and concepts of selling will necessarily have to change. We'll look carefully into the means by which we can, individually, share in the improved selling results this change will bring.

Next, we will delineate our natural talents and skills and actually effect a personal inventory. In this manner we can critically appraise the personal tools we have to work with so that later we can fill in the bare spots in order to achieve better sales performance.

Then we will move forward to a new conception of a higher level of selling—not just improved selling but actually a different way to sell. You will accomplish this metamorphosis a little at a time until eventually most of the things you now do will be changed to a more dynamic selling procedure. Each change will bring with it better immediate results. Your goal will be to adapt your whole sales effort perfectly to the wants and needs of each individual customer, to each individual selling situation.

This journey could be considered an adventure. It isn't—simply because the end results (higher performance, more earnings, and greater personal growth opportunity) are too predictable. But by thoughtfully reasoning our way to greater profits through "Ingenious Selling," this journey can be an enjoyable and profitable experience.

A Look at Selling in a New Light

The selling profession has not kept pace with a dramatic marketing and merchandising evolution, nor with consumers' vastly changed buying habits; and yet, the individual salesman has done a creditable job of self-training and development with the knowledge and tools he has had to work with. Most of what is currently described as sales training, although basically sound, is quite impractical in coping with today's selling problems.

The fact is that training for the selling profession must be almost wholly self-development. This is not true of other professions. The accountant has his well-documented procedures, the lawyer his briefs, and the doctor his journals. The salesman, however, has only the background of his experience, plus possibly a company "course" in sales training.

Today a different kind of selling is necessary. Everything points up the fact that a vastly greater volume of goods can be sold and absorbed at all levels by consumers. It is entirely possible for the salesman to get more and bigger orders and, at the same time, accomplish great economic good for our whole system.

The salesman who learns what this different kind of selling is and how to apply it to his job will enjoy improved sales results for the short range, and greater opportunity for personal promotion over the longer period. However, the methods for learning these new techniques and the skills required in today's selling must follow an approach which differs widely from the step-by-step formula of stereotyped sales training.

Why must selling be so different in order to capitalize on today's opportunities? There are, in fact, multiple reasons. It is surely obvious that more products can be absorbed by consumers, but they are not. Is this simply because consumers won't buy? Actually, they are eager to buy. Is marketing not alert to the opportunity? Great prosperity is so evident that marketing would be stupid not to recognize it and create well-designed plans for it. The answer is in the practice of selling, and the present practice of selling is just not getting the job accomplished. Let's start our examination of the reasons why selling methods must change.

The Problem of Product Selection

We recognize there are a great variety of products and great numbers of products within each variety from which consumers may make selections. An average drug store, for example, will carry some 27,000 different items. A big candy counter in a department store, supermarket or drug store will show at least a hundred varieties of candy, with several brands for most of the varieties. There is great variety and brand selection in toothbrushes, cosmetics, lingerie, hair preparations, sport shirts, neckties, plastic tape, hand tools, fish hooks, automobiles.

Suppose you represent a manufacturer of tape—masking tape, mending tape, industrial tape, electric tape, etc. How does the consumer even find your product, let alone buy it? Your answer should be, "Because of *me*—I'm here only because I can get my products the kind of exposure that will sell them."

Let's consider as another example any grocery supermarket product. No promotional ideas, no matter how original, nor displays that are a result of commercial artists' and copywriters' fondest dreams, all backed by big advertising, will move products that have either poor location in the store or inadequate shelf space, or both. Only an "on-the-spot" salesman can get the location or space, and then police it for his company.

When the salesman is in the store he can recognize in a flash what should be done to enable his product to sell better. But how to get this accomplished? As Hamlet says, "That is the question." This requires ingenuity in selling, and the techniques must be new and different. The problem in this instance is not, "Will the retailer buy the product?" but, "Will it move?" and, "How can it be given a chance to move?" All the advice ever written on how to get attention and how to close the sale won't solve that problem. Something new must be added.

We have always assumed that our job as salesmen was to get orders. And, of course, that *is* exactly the end result. But our selling techniques might actually have to be directed to getting better display space, i.e., consumer attention, for our products at the point of sale. There is a difference of direction involved in an approach to convince the buyer to stock a new untried product, as against convincing him to give a product he knows will sell better display.

Now, the fact that there are multitudes of products of all kinds from multitudes of companies, all backed with good promotion, good display and advertising, makes it very difficult for each company's salesmen to get the most desirable location and shelf space. Certainly good merchandising tools are necessary, but the salesman who relies upon his company's program alone will lose business in today's market without even knowing it.

Texts on selling are inclined to skim over this tremendous problem of consumer selection in products and services. Yet this is a very big factor in how the salesman directs his effort—how he allocates his time, how he plans his calls, how he organizes his routing. It is certainly apparent why many, many categories of selling must change if only to meet this one condition.

A company's sales programs and promotions are only as good as the interpretation given them by the salesman for each individual retailer's needs. We do not imply here that the proper presentation of a good sales program will not get an order. It usually does get an order—but often the order doesn't represent the potential. Without a new approach which takes into account the great selection of products and services available to the consumer, business is lost—and yet the salesman feels only success. This is very costly. Now, let's explore another reason why selling will undergo change.

The Problem of Consumer Attention

Today's competition for the consumer's attention in advertising is fantastic. The cost of television time and print space on a national basis is so high that only the multi-billion companies can really stop and hold the consumer's eye for product identification. And even the multi-billion companies are consumer hungry without good point-of-sale tie-up.

No one will dispute the power of advertising. It is a strong weapon in any promotional portfolio, regardless of the product or size of the company. The facts are, however, that there are mighty few companies who can rely solely on advertising to move their products. Tobacco? Certainly not, there are just too many brands, as attested to by the number of tobacco wholesalers and direct company display men and salesmen. Soap and detergents? Here again, new products and multiple brands require combination display men and order-getting salesmen.

Automobile companies are an exception to this precept because they have exclusive sales agencies—and that makes a difference. Automobiles are big ticket sales and enjoy a consumer fascination unequaled by other products. Yet, in spite of all of these advantages, General Motors, Ford and Chrysler maintain very aggressive sales organizations to put pressure on their dealerships as well as to help them with their selling problems.

It becomes plain that advertising is not strong enough to stand alone as a selling tool even for the giants of industry. For the myriad of companies who advertise substantially it can be relied upon only lightly. The consumer is inundated with advertising messages, and he can't possibly absorb them all.

Because of this advertising dilution, most companies are in the unenviable position of having to depend upon their sales forces to get much of the consumers' sales attention for them— unenviable because in too many instances this means unpredictable point-of-sale tie-up. Unpredictable because salesmen are, by and large, staying with the obsolete sales habit of depending solely upon their company's advertising to entice the retailer to give them good display. These salesmen have learned to get the order and get out of the store. Because they do not get display, they ignore great potential.

Because advertising cannot possibly do the job it once could do, a different and more predictable kind of selling is evolving. Companies are aware of the new emphasis that must be placed at the doorstep of their sales departments. Yet these new techniques and skills are something company sales training courses really cannot give to the salesman; this training is actually something that only the salesman can give to himself.

The Problem of Consumer Convenience

Today, the American consumer is King and shopping habits have greatly changed over the past ten years. We have an economy of abundance. We are in a perpetual buyers' market. It is a paradox that man throughout the ages has struggled for comfort and convenience and now that he has it in vast measure there is even greater competition for what comfort and convenience he chooses to accept. Convenience itself as a consumer benefit has become the greatest motivating force in the selection of consumer products. To identify a few "conveniences" that have become necessities: (1) Automobiles—automatic shifting, power steering, power brakes, power windows, power radio aerials, door and trunk releases—even cruiseomatic controls so that you don't have to press on the gas pedal! (2) Ballpoint pens don't require that you take off and put on a pen cap, (3) Electric knives, can openers, toothbrushes, dishwashers, (4) Aerosol deodorants, bug killers, floor polishes, paint, automatic garage doors.

Certainly the salesman must be keenly aware of the great potential available to him in this growing consumer interest in convenience. A few years ago convenience was not even listed as a buying appeal, while today it is probably the single most important reason why consumers buy.

Yet this matter of convenience, in another form, represents another concept for the salesman to consider. In England people have great patience for standing in line for the things they want, and they will come back the next day for another wait if need be. The American consumer would rather pass it up than wait. American business is well aware of this fact. Nowhere on earth is the consumer catered to as he is in the United States. *It is not enough that the salesman sell his product to a turnover conscious retailer, but he must sell it in quantities and in a manner that will guarantee the product will be available to consumers who won't go to any inconvenience to get it.* Actually, this indisputable fact spells more potential for better selling.

The quest for greater comfort and convenience has also translated itself into a great change in consumers' shopping habits. Keeping pace with new consumer habits in shopping offers a great untapped opportunity for most salesmen in consumer goods lines. Let us explore this new direction in shopping habits by explaining first that there is very little "direct" shopping in today's market place. By "direct" we mean a consumer who wants or needs a certain product of a certain brand and who makes a special single shopping effort to get it.

An example of a "direct" shopper is a confirmed smoker who makes a special trip to the store for a favorite brand of cigarettes. Today even this shopper, although he still may make a special trip, will swich if his favorite brand is not available.

There are very few branded products that receive so-called "direct" shopping attention from the consumer. Rather, consumers tuck away in their minds their want or need for a product and it doesn't come out until they are on a shopping trip. They see the product displayed and they make the purchase. Convenience of shopping, i.e., locations of stores in shopping centers, easy "serve yourself" access to merchandise, abundance of products in super stores, all these things have prompted the consumer to put off buying necessities until it is convenient to do so. The shopper doesn't make a list any more, he just browses through stores and picks up the things that he has previously made up his mind to buy—plus a few extras.

An example of this is in the writing instrument business. Ten years ago when a consumer needed or wanted a quality higher-priced writing instrument, he made a special trip to get it. This was classed as a "direct" or "on purpose" consumer purchase. Today he "lets it go" until during a customary shopping trip he is attracted to a writing instrument department. A bell rings in his mind and he goes over to the counter to make a selection.

There is an important aspect of this obsolete so-called direct sale of a writing instrument to the consumer. Those same ten years ago when a consumer thought of buying a quality writing instrument he thought of a higher priced fountain pen—$5.00

and up. Today the ballpoint pen has been perfected with good quality at $1.98. Even when they are priced at 19¢, most pens will write satisfactorily for a time. In other words, the abundance of products available at lower prices has discouraged the consumer from making a special effort to look for exactly what he wants, even if he has a special brand definitely in mind.

In this situation a quality writing instrument manufacturer, by advertising, and by his own stature in the marketplace, can induce consumers' thought-process toward his product, and yet his competitor, just by having better display at the point of sale, can switch the consumer purchase. The competitor reaps an unearned reward. Obviously, then, this situation requires well-trained and alert salesmen who are creative enough to translate the company's promotions and advertising into consumer sales of the company's products through their retailers —salesmen who will police their companies' interests in the retail store. It sounds like a mouthful, but the lesson is clear and simple: Salesmen are more vital today than ever before.

Americans who have recently lived in England report that someday the new supermarkets which are currently appearing throughout that country will greatly change British shopping habits. But the time apparently is not yet. It seems that the Britisher is still a "direct" buyer. He goes to a green grocer if he wants vegetables and fruit; to a meat market for meat; to a bakery for baked goods; and on and on. The English tend to shop only for what they are after and this habit is transferred to the new supermarkets, with the result that their cash registers, as contrasted with those in the United States, ring up pretty skimpy amounts.

The United States was pretty much like this only twelve to fifteen years ago, but now the so-called direct shopper of this bygone period has all but disappeared and so also have the precepts of marketing and merchandising of that era. It is woefully apparent why the selling techniques and skills required for today's selling challenges must be different from those of the past. Companies of every description need reawakened selling effort at all levels to further company growth. No company is going anywhere without increased sales, and to sell in what appears to be saturated markets requires real creative selling. The individual salesman who meets this challenge will get an increased standard of living for his greater productiveness.

Thousands of product categories that were once classed as "considered" purchases by consumers are now classed as "impulse" purchases. Most housewives, for example, still make a supermarket shopping list. But let's say your wife decided upon roast beef for Sunday dinner. She is attracted to a display of canned hams and changes her mind. On impulse she gives the business to another meat packer. In an old-fashioned meat market this would not have happened. Grocery buying once was almost 100% considered—often the purchase was made over the telephone. Today it is almost all impulse.

Is buying a greeting card a deliberate purchase? You would think so. Yet card rack operators report many buyers simply "stop off" and pick up an assortment of cards for future use. They don't even know who they're going to send them to. Stop to think about it, you send the same Christmas card to many people, so why not the same "get well" or birthday card?

You are building a little something in the basement and you need about a quarter pound of three penny nails. Sure as anything you'll come home with an assortment of all sizes of nails. It's just too convenient to buy them "while you're there." You've always got 'em if you need 'em.

Now if you are a "nail salesman" there's only one way to increase your business and that is to take advantage of the *impulse* purchase that was once a considered purchase only.

The transfer of the "considered" purchase to one now classed as "impulse" is but another symptom of the great transformation of living conditions and habits. For our purposes here, we don't have to concern ourselves as to why consumers' conditions and habits have changed but only to recognize that they are changed. Then we should ask ourselves, "Has my selling changed with these conditions? Has the total selling function changed? Not marketing or merchandising, but the very act of selling itself—the process of selling, the techniques and skills used in selling by the individual salesman?" The answer is, "No." The salesman today is acting and doing and saying things in much the same fashion as his counterpart of thirty years ago. Moreover, the salesman is being instructed at every turn to act and do and say things in an apparently ageless selling manner.

Selling Defined

Now, as mentioned, we are not discussing marketing and merchandising techniques which actually are greatly altered from the past. We are concerned only with selling itself. So, for the purposes of this book:

> *Marketing* is defined as the *total function* of bringing goods and services from their usable or finished state to the ultimate consumer.
> *Merchandising* can be described as the *ways and means* which assist the performance of the marketing function, such as programs, plans, displays and dispensers, promotions, offers.
> *Selling is the act of arranging for the exchange or transfer of goods and services for money,* as an end result of the marketing function.

Great strides in statistical information via computers and data processing have been a boon to marketing people. They can formulate plans and arrive at decisions more accurately and quickly than ever before.

Merchandising people understand the consumer, his wants and needs and how to appeal to him for favorable results. Vast changes have emerged in merchandising techniques.

But everything funnels through sales. If the wholesaler or distributor doesn't buy properly, or if the retailer doesn't buy and display properly, there is a great loss of thrust for the marketing and merchandising effort, and a great loss of revenue for the company—all adding up to increased opportunity for the salesman.

Marketers with the wherewithal often stimulate sales with saturation advertising to consumers. They create demand and force sales through the retailer. Over a long period, however, this effort is difficult to sustain and such marketers eventually must turn to the sales force. Competition sees to it that products have good value. High quality production costs and high advertising costs preclude employing these "advertising-to-force-sales" methods on a continuing basis.

"Look," says management, "you've got to have a sales force anyway. Make them responsible now. Cut the advertising. Cut the free goods offers. Make certain that you have a well-trained, well-supervised sales force. Let's make some profit on this product."

Is this unreasonable? Not at all. A product of value that will move because of big advertising will move with minimal advertising. But not if the sales force does not adjust accordingly. Consumers have found a want or need for the product and it is no less because the advertising is reduced. If it often appears that consumers' want or need is diminished, it is only because salesmen are not of a talent level to assume this full responsibility.

Sales managers and salesmen don't like this kind of talk. It is only natural to want heavy advertising support and superior merchandising tools. The more the merrier—and the easier the task. But let's face it, field selling, the actual meeting of salesman and buyer, must carry its full share of the burden, i.e., opportunity for the professional salesman. Advertising and merchandising help must remain within limits of profitability. The field sales force must assume its rightful responsibility.

In some areas of selling, advertising departments act as the sales department via direct mail. Your first reaction, if you are calling on retailers, might be that this is a "direct to consumer" operation and doesn't affect you. However, ask yourself this question, "Why doesn't this manufacturer go through retailers?" These are the reasons:

1. The retailer won't give the kind of selling support necessary to do a good job. In other words, the manufacturer believes that if he uses a sales force it won't be

effective in getting the point-of-sale job accomplished. This is an indictment on the power of personal selling and it indicates that selling techniques must change.

2. The cost of selling is too high. But if direct mail is a less costly way of selling percentage-wise, this again is an indictment on personal selling as a volume producer. Certainly this too is an indication that selling must undergo change to meet the challenge.

Of course, the facts are that personal selling has accepted the lion's share of responsibilities in the total marketing function— and successfully. The U. S. economy didn't reach boom proportions with selling falling down on the job. However, if we ask if selling is now performing at a level in keeping with the huge, and growing, potential, that's something else again.

There are two problems inherent with selling in capitalizing on the situation:

1. Selling involves an individual called a salesman who *should* act and react differently than all others in the business profession.
2. Selling most closely involves a human relationship which, in turn, involves elements that vary and change constantly.

No two salesmen are alike and no two selling situations are the same. In fact, selling situations are growing more and more *dissimilar all the time,* and salesmen will need to become more individualistic in their approach to these conditions.

At this point, let's review what we have been talking about and determine if we are getting anywhere.

1. We've discussed the evolution of change. Consumers' altered buying habits, and consumers' capacity to absorb more products and services is a change. The great new variety of products and the new methods of distributing them to consumers is a change. *There is more competition for consumers' attention at the point of*

sale. The already high and increasing cost of getting product identification through advertising is a change. Consumers' shopping habits (as distinguished from buying habits) have changed. The "considered" consumer purchase as distinguished from the "impulse" consumer purchase has changed.

2. Marketing and merchandising techniques have frequently kept up with these changes. Salesmen's individual selling techniques often have not. The very act of selling—what the salesman does, how he acts and reacts, what he says and how he says it—these things have not changed. Selling has *not* moved ahead with its opportunity and its potential.

3. Because of the individualistic and human factors involved, and because sales knowledge cannot be documented as is a medical journal or a legal brief, selling depends entirely upon *individual knowledge and experience*. Therefore, selling cannot simply be taught; it must be learned through self-development.

All of this chapter has outlined the basis for this book. There are tremendous new opportunities open to the field salesman if he but recognizes what they are and learns how to exploit them. At the same time, companies have explored virtually all avenues of growth through the application of marketing and merchandising techniques. They are looking for self-trained salesmen who with newly developed selling techniques can produce greater volume from a static sales area or situation.

A company can acquaint a salesman with the advantages and vulnerabilities of its products, and can explain its policies, merchandising programs, and advertising and promotional plans. How well the salesman presents these facts to his buyers, what he says and how he says it, how well he is organized to accomplish his total assignment, how much of his own personal flavor he adds to the recipe, these are elements of his own ingenuity.

The marketplace is not the same today as it was yesterday.

It will not be the same tomorrow as it is today. The alert salesman finds within the situation great opportunity. This book is intended to enable you to realize that opportunity by helping you to sharpen your talents and skills for greater results through new techniques in learning and the ingenious application of these newfound techniques.

2

Introduction to
Personal Development in
The Art of Ingenious Selling

The most important difference between success and mediocrity is an elusive element called ingenuity. The dictionary defines it as the quality of having inventive power: cleverness in contriving or originating. It goes on to say, "Ingenuity is inferior to genius, being rather mechanical than creative and is shown in devising expedients, overcoming difficulties, adapting means to ends." Synonyms include acuteness, cleverness, inventiveness, readiness, and skill.

Everybody of average intelligence and ability has ingenuity to a degree. Choosing a career in selling and being able to stick with it attests to more than ordinary powers of ingeniousness. The trick is to develop and employ this inherent trait as the powerful asset it is in the field of selling. There are sure-fire ways to do it.

Let's take first things first and examine some examples of ingenuity in selling:

Some years ago a big new business was emerging in the cosmetic field. It was the home permanent wave, and many new suppliers were entering the burgeoning market. One such company had developed a product which we will call "Swirl and Curl" and was represented in a Pennsylvania territory by a young and aggressive salesman whom we will name Tom Baker. Tom Baker had a problem.

Fact No. 1—the application of ingeniousness always stems from problems. Ingeniousness is a problem-solving device.

Tom Baker had covered his territory, consisting of drug store and department store cosmetic departments, only twice. His company had been advertising Swirl and Curl heavily, his "point-of-purchase" material was effective, and Swirl and Curl was selling well; but now, on only the third time around, Tom Baker was hearing complaints.

Women were bringing Swirl and Curl back to cosmetic counters for exchange for other products. They explained that Swirl and Curl did not produce the advertised tight curls. Specifically, it left milady's hair "too loose, too fluffy." Already some of Tom Baker's customers had returned stock to the wholesaler. Although inventories were low, other retailers "just wanted to wait" before placing fill-in orders.

A few discreet telephone calls within the company revealed that two older salesmen in adjoining territories had quit. But company bulletins continued only to stress the strong advertising campaign and seemed to be oblivious of this new and growing problem. Tom telephoned his immediate supervisor to no avail. It was obvious that he had problems of his own. In fact, the more calls Tom Baker made the more it appeared to him that the handwriting was on the wall.

Fact No. 2—there is always a "moment of truth" before ingeniousness can take over. This manifests itself in whether the salesman resolves to tackle the problem or to avoid it.

Tom Baker decided to read and reread his company's and his competitor's advertisements. They all seemed to extol the same features. He talked to behind-the-counter sales people who reported that women selected home permanents without much "pre-sell" on their part. But these same women customers complained bitterly if the product didn't act as they thought it was supposed to—and Swirl and Curl just didn't produce tight curls.

Fact No. 3—before a problem can be solved, you must know what it is. In this instance investigation revealed that the problem was not the salesman's ineffectiveness but rather a product deficiency. Or was it?

Tom Baker developed a simple, new pitch. Let us outline it:

Retailer: I don't need any Swirl and Curl right now. In fact, I'm thinking of returning my stock. I had three complaints this week that your home permanent just doesn't produce tight curls— my customers tell me it leaves their hair wavy enough but too fluffy.

Tom Baker: You know, Mr. Druggist, I'm only sorry that I didn't give you all of the product facts on Swirl and Curl. Actually, Swirl and Curl is the only product made to give the soft, feminine, casual look to hair. It doesn't leave hair hard and brittle. This is a new look that's sweeping the country. You will do your customers a service to tell them this when they buy Swirl and Curl.

Retailer: What of those who bring it back? Some are regular and old customers.

Tom Baker: Exchange it for another package and tell them to use it exactly as directed and to expect a different, more exciting hair style—more appealing and younger looking. Then if your customers don't like the product they can try something else.

Retailer: Okay, fill me in, and we'll see what happens.

So what happened? The same presentation worked in forty-five calls that week. In two weeks, Tom Baker had retraced his steps. The heavy advertising would have moved merchandise and if there were still problems, he might as well know it. On the first call, no complaints—sales good. In fact, only five accounts had problems, and these could be traced to earlier sales. Besides, the retailers were happy and were now pushing Swirl and Curl as a new style in home permanents.

Note that Tom Baker actually had an in-store promotion going for him. To solve a complaint problem he had counter display plus clerk support or even recommendation. He probably couldn't have bought that kind of support without the problem.

Tom Baker telephoned the product manager at headquarters and explained what had happened. The word got through to marketing management. Advertising and packaging were changed, a new appeal was discovered, the field force was immediately updated, a product was saved—possibly even the company.

Fact No. 4—many times a factory or headquarter problem is a field problem after all. Here a salesman was promoted for turning a liability into an asset—by employing ingenious selling.

A lucky coincidence? Not at all. Any smart salesman can increase his daily earnings and his chances for promotion by learning how to apply the natural characteristic of ingenuity to his selling. There are multitudes of ways. Let's look at the one we've just discussed—turning a liability into an asset.

A supermarket complains of bent cans. The salesman remarks: "You know what you should do? You ought to have a big Bent Can Sale once a month—two cents off on every bent can. You would have people searching them out—you would get people into the store and sell lots of extra merchandise. This could be a big promotion. In fact if you try it, the next time you'll be ordering them bent."

Suppose your competitor is claiming that his whidget makes a half turn and yours does not. That's no deficiency in your product. You just don't have another mechanical part to go wrong and cause trouble. You state it positively, however: "In this product there are a minimum of moving parts to fail and cause costly delays."

Turning liabilities into assets can become powerful tools in anyone's sales technique. Here are a few suggestions on how to begin using ingenious techniques for greater immediate results:

1. List product features your competitors have that you don't have and then devise reasons why your product is better without them. This is not intended to imply that you are being invited to knock your competitors' products. You don't have to do that. On the other hand, you just can't wait for a clue from your customer

in order to bring the subject up for discussion. Tactfully include these "liabilities turned to assets" in your planned presentation to your customer without competitor mention.

Mr. Dealer, you've probably wondered why we don't have _____ _____ _____ in our product. (Now give a positive reason why your product is better without it.)

Example: Mr. Dealer, you've undoubtedly noticed that we don't use _____ _____ _____. We feel this is unsure and untried. We hesitate to put you in a defensive situation by using it, especially since you are doing so well with the line.

Example: Mr. Dealer, our design is the standard of the industry, accepted by everyone. It has been satisfactory, and as your repeat business depends upon customer satisfaction, I feel sure that you will. . . .

2. It would be well to keep in mind that your competitor's salesman is not asleep either and that he is very possibly using some of these very same techniques concerning your products. So if your product has certain advantages over his, it would be well to recognize the fact that he has probably made a few points in selling against you. If he has scored, here is an example of a rebuttal:

Mr. Dealer, I couldn't help but notice your counter display of _____ _____ _____. In checking your stock I find that, in spite of our second-place display position in your store, the demand for our product is better than ever. I can predict even greater sales for you because of the public acceptance of our new advertised feature, _____ _____ _____. Seriously, the time has come for you to trade display positions for these products.

3. Now let's look further into this product area of turning liabilities into assets which resolves itself around the complaints you receive from your retailers or your wholesalers. Sit down right now and list your product

complaints and then answer these complaints by using the "liability turned to asset" technique. Here is an example:

Retailer: I have had several customer complaints lately that your _____ fountain pen is writing much too heavily and that in some cases it leaks.

Salesman: That's bad, Mr. Dealer, but really not serious. Actually, a fountain pen wouldn't write if it didn't leak—it is a controlled leaking device. Now, I recognize that a pen that leaks is certainly not efficient, but if it doesn't leak it won't write at all, and a pen that won't write at all represents the really major deficiency. Let me show you a few simple things that you can do. (Explain the few simple corrections toward making a pen operate more efficiently.)

There's nothing like a smile and a helping hand to bring a customer back often. *In fact, that's the reason I've thought that you should promote a Pen Clinic and advertise it, to bring in these ready-made customers to your pen counters.* People just don't take care of their pens these days, and you ought to capitalize on it.

Another example:

Retailer: I've had several customers tell me that your cough syrup just isn't effective—doesn't seem to be strong enough.

Salesman: Some people expect a cough syrup to cure a cold—that it be rough and tough. Nothing can do that. In fact, no cough syrup is effective in all instances. Our product is designed especially for women and children for whom a rough remedy would have unpleasant after-effects.

This syrup is gentle and soothing, and over the years you have had multitudes of regular users to every complainer. This is a cough syrup you can prescribe with confidence—confident that it does what we say it will do in by far the majority of instances.

And another:

Retailer: Your competitor proved to me that your rubber bands were not "supple." He showed me by demonstrating how his rubber bands floated on a glass of water—other rubber bands, including yours, sank to the bottom of the glass.

Salesman: Well, he was right about one thing, our rubber bands don't float—in fact, most of our customers never float them. But our bands do stretch, hold tight, and last. We use the best latex rubber for elasticity and tensile strength. These bands do what they are supposed to do—stretch, hold longer, and last longer. Don't let your customers be the goat in this kind of a phony demonstration.

And still another:

Retailer: Your camera doesn't have "X" and "X" features as does your competitor's camera.

Salesman: Actually, the majority of your customers want a camera that takes good, clear pictures easily. With them, it's a hobby, not a profession. Really, you'll get more customer dissatisfaction from cameras that your customers don't learn to use properly. Let's go over the features of our camera that have made it so popular with your customers.

We have explored one aspect of ingenious selling—turning liabilities into assets. We discovered ways and means of applying this technique by, first, comparing our product features with competitors' product features and, second, listing product complaints. In both instances we devised the actual selling sentences which can be tucked away in the back of our minds to use as the occasion arises.

Before we leave this intriguing subject for other applications of ingenious selling, there is another area where converting a liability into an asset eases the path to a sale. That area is company policies.

The credit policy of your company is based upon good business principles. Prompt collections reduce costs. Longer terms and datings will induce higher costs of business operation— interest costs. Very possibly longer credit terms are required in your operation as a competitive weapon but, remember, if they are used their cost will result in something taken away from such aids as merchandising helps, promotion, advertising, or even commissions.

Generally, the shorter your terms and datings as compared

to your competitor's, the better your competitive position. If your competitor gives longer terms or better cash discounts, you can almost bet that your product turns faster and has a better consumer brand image. Now, if your customers have made a liability out of your credit policies, it's about time that you turned them into an asset. Try this:

> Mr. Dealer, discipline is good for all of us. It's my job to help you buy in direct relation to turnover so that you can realize the best profit on my line.

> The reason my competitor's terms are longer is that their line doesn't move as fast as mine. That has to be the answer. So, if you are doing as well or better with my competitor as you are with me because of his terms, you are actually losing sales and profits by bucking the trend—in other words, forcing substitutions for my line.

> We've got to get you back into a position where you'll actually invite shorter terms to keep you in a good buying condition in order to take advantage of your faster turnover.

Too many salesmen look upon many of their company's policies as hurdles which they must endure because they are seemingly necessary in overall company operation. These salesmen treat their company policies as liabilities to sales and, worst of all, they let their customers treat them as liabilities. They fail to see that the reason for policies is almost always positive. In other words, these policies have been assets all along—and from the customer's point of view, too. But they must be explained properly.

You might go through the most seemingly objectionable policy positions of your company. List them, and then use a little ingenuity in turning them into assets. Examples to look for, in addition to credit, terms, and discounts might be: freight and delivery policies, returned merchandise policies, and consumer price maintenance policies.

Think of it this way: Your position must be a competitive one or you will not realize your true sales potential. Undoubtedly, there are policies in your company that are outdated and archaic and which ought to be revised. Nevertheless, the sale is now. You've got a lot of living to do, mouths to feed, payments to make, savings to accumulate. The application of ingenuity toward turning these seemingly disadvantageous policies into assets is the immediate answer to greater sales right now.

Turning liabilities into assets represents a powerful technique in practicing the art of ingenious selling. It guarantees to turn "no's" into "yes's" and to close more immediate sales. Moreover, its application is a great self-development technique in a successful selling career. So now let's move on and examine another strong weapon to help us become not just better, but more ingenious salesmen.

A successful salesman has to be "fast on his feet," so to speak. He has to be able to sense the proper direction of the sale. If one plan is not going too well, he must quickly change direction without letting the sales presentation get out of hand. Treating the sales presentation as a "sales discussion" or even a "sales conversation" is the clue. We have talked of the sales interview as being "directed conversation." Unless the customer gets into the act, there is no way of knowing how well the sale is going at any given point. This is a separate subject and is examined in another chapter. For the moment, we must assume that we are in control of the sales interview, and we sense that the sale is not going too well. How do we change direction, and how do we determine that we are on the right track?

We shall describe this technique in the art of ingenious selling as the "Big Switch," and it is not a spur of the moment thing at all. It is thoroughly planned in advance.

Here are a few truisms:

• A buyer may like to hear a good story or tell about his fishing exploits, but he buys only for the effect on his pocketbook.

• The employee buyer risks his job unless he thinks of the firm rather than his personal likes and dislikes. He thinks sales.

• The owner buyer risks his business unless he thinks of the firm rather than his personal likes and dislikes. He thinks profits.

• Emotionalism plays a big part in any sale because it sets the mood for the sale. But it must revolve around the pocketbook.

• The most effective salesman in a territory is not necessarily the best liked but rather the one who is making the most money for his dealers.

It is elementary that a person buys either for himself or for others in order to satisfy a want or a need. No sale is ever made until the salesman discovers what that want or need is and convinces the buyer that what he is offering will satisfy that want or need.

We don't imply that this happens in every selling situation. In the greatest number of transactions the buyer simply knows what he wants and buys it. In these instances no sale is made. And yet many salesmen actually live off these transactions day in and day out, really never making a sale but simply permitting the buyer to buy.

Is this bad? Not at all so long as the buyer buys properly and so long as the salesman realizes a fulfillment of his real opportunity. Too many times, however, these things just don't come about. The buyer buys improperly and the salesman loses potential—all because the salesman has lost control of the interview.

But we're talking about sales and selling opportunities. *This requires control of the interview, as we've said, and the first requirement to accomplish that is understanding the buyer's wants and needs.* In selling the vast panorama of consumer products to retailers or wholesalers, the overall objective (need or want) is quite simple—profit. Specifically—greater sales and profits. More specifically—more dollars in sales and profits.

Now, our subject here is using ingenuity, and we are rapidly getting to an absorbing application of it. When you are selling, keep thinking about sales, profits, and money for your customer. Whenever you sense the sale is drifting, think of sales, profits, and money, and get back on the track—abruptly.

Mr. Dealer, let's get back to (diversionary subject) in a moment. Right now, I would like to clarify my proposition in its true perspective of bringing more dollars of sales and profits to you. . . .

Now comes the "Big Switch"—your application of ingenious selling. The application of your proposition, your product, to greater dollar sales and profits—more money in the till for your customer. It will be necessary to do some beforehand thinking:

1. If your product is of high quality and high price, stress that concentration and good display will increase turnover, and thus sales and profits, faster than in any other way.
2. If your product is of good quality but has a lower price, stress high turnover possibilities on a low cost "sell itself" basis.

Oddly enough, both of the above situations can be supported with plenty of proof—and you should have it. Set up the "ideal situation" test with several of your retailers for a certain time period and make sure that accurate day-to-day records are kept. After the time period has expired, the retailer will want to continue with the "test" to keep up his own sales. Now you have factual sales evidence plus a "sold" retailer who will continue to supply you with sales ammunition.

Some successful salesmen run continuing or periodical "tests" with every important account in their territories. They continue to build their own sales testimonials. A retailer once said of such a salesman: "He's sometimes insulting, and he never buys a lunch. But he's welcome in my store whenever he comes around because he's making money for me. And he's proved it over and over again."

So we turn to the "Big Switch." We move beyond the place where other salesmen move off. During the presentation we have shown the advertising, the point-of-sale pieces, the products themselves, and we've asked for the order with remarks such as, "I would suggest now that we put the bulk of the stock in the stores with a minimum back-up in the warehouse," or, "Of the two displays, the No. 940 seems to me to fit your operation best." Note that even disagreement with these closing statements means that the buyer is willing to place the order. In other words, we try for the "automatic" order.

But, we fail. So, instead of closing again and even again, we employ the "Big Switch."

> Mr. Dealer, I am going to prove to you, in a two-weeks' test right on your own counters, that you can increase your dollar profits 33⅓% with this line. All you have to do is follow the simple example of _____ _____. Here's what he did and here are the results he got. (Show your test dealer results.) I could give you a dozen more just like it. Now here's what you need to get started on the road to higher sales and profits.

The "Big Switch" is a documentation of retailer successes with your product line and is employed only when you need it to insure the tough sale. It represents, first, an understanding of the raw basic want or need, and, then, application at just the right moment. It takes a very adamant buyer to turn down a "sure thing." And proved opportunity is a sure thing. This process is practicing the art of ingenious selling.

There is just no substitute for ingeniousness in selling. You can follow all of the rules made and you will never really improve your sales averages and take advantage of your sales opportunities consistently unless you apply the art of ingenious selling. This requires thought and analysis—in advance. Occasionally you may stumble upon an ingenious answer on the spur of the moment that solves a problem sale. But you can't depend upon it. Too many salesmen expect "something to come to them," and it just really never comes.

Yet, it's not just a matter of planning the call in advance. Planning is a prerequisite to every call. Practicing the art of ingenious selling goes much deeper because it involves creativity, uniqueness, and a different approach to effect the sale. It can be applied to all areas of the selling function.

• It may involve a different way of routing to expose your offer strategically to specific accounts after one competitor's salesman and before another.

• It may be the means to accomplish certain planning or analyzing chores while waiting for calls, thus conserving time.

• It could involve a means for reducing the number of call-backs and/or making the call-back do double duty.

• It could be a better way to handle reports and other paper work for more effective use of time.

• It might be a new method of using sample equipment or visual aids to get bigger orders.

All of these things, and many others which we will treat in subsequent chapters, are subjects for practicing the art of ingenious selling—an important key to a successful sales career. As you have been reading this chapter certain ideas have occurred to you. Turn back and make notes so that later you can refer to them in developing and applying your own talents for ingenious selling.

3

How to Acquire the Fundamental Skills for Ingenious Selling Through the Technique Of Everyday Awareness

Many salesmen in their respective fields, mainly by virtue of their own experience, have kept close pace with the advanceing marketing and merchandising techniques of the companies they work for. Because of advertising, sales programs and promotions, and normal company growth patterns, plus good application of these things, these salesmen have enjoyed relatively high success. Yet even for these top performers there is enormous new potential by the power use of their undiscovered inherent selling talents. Imagine what that potential can be for the "average" salesman!

In Chapter 1 we set a strong foundation for a positive conclusion, namely, that new approaches for learning how to do a better job of selling must be devised. The first of these new approaches in acquiring the skills required for ingenious selling is mastering a technique called awareness.

Being "aware" would be possessing knowledge of some fact or action—being conscious or cognizant. Awareness is, in the sense we define it, an understanding in our own best individual interests of the things that are going on around us. Once we develop in our everyday living a sense of awareness of the things that will benefit us in our profession of selling, then we have a vast new area for learning other than just from our work experience.

Let's take a homely example: You have just returned from a personal business visit to the local bank:

Your wife: What's going on at the bank, Charlie?

You: What usually goes on at a bank? Some people are putting money in, others are taking it out.

Your wife: Oh.

You flick on the TV.

Or:

Your wife: What's going on at the bank, Charlie?

You: You know, Flo, that bank is twice as crowded as it was a year ago on Friday nights. I must have waited ten minutes to get to a window. There are more people coming into this area and there's more business being done. People around here are carrying a lot of cash and that represents discretionary spending. The cash discount stores and variety stores are crowded. I can use this with my dealers. I also noticed that Will Jones was getting another loan and his business is on short-term credit. That means he must be doing real well as he needs inventory. You know he carries a competitive line to our whidgets so I'd better find out what he's doing that my dealer isn't doing.

Your wife: Oh.

You still flick on the TV. (But you've already made written notes for "follow up" action.)

If you were a stockbroker and you read an article in *Life* about how West Coast fashions were sweeping the country's teen-age market, you'd quickly check up on textile companies located on the West Coast. Why? Obviously, to see if there were capital gains possibilities in these industry stocks.

A doctor might be quite interested to observe that a smoke

and soot smog seemed to be developing in his area as some new industry moved in. Such knowledge could help his correct diagnosis batting average.

To an insurance agent, a real estate broker, a banker, to name a few, awareness in everyday living is a way of life. Almost everything they see around them they can translate to business use. A new highway, a new subdivision, a vacant building, a change in traffic routing, and many, many other daily elements can create opportunities and affect decisions. They can gain these "awareness" impressions playing golf, at cocktail parties, on a Sunday drive, reading the paper. It is quite obvious that in these professions the work pattern is not an eight to five proposition.

However, most of these professional people just don't make full use of their awareness opportunities any more than do most classes of salesmen. Work is work, leisure is leisure, living is living, and that's it. It's only an accident if something from social or leisure observance affects a part of the work pattern of most salesmen.

An ingenious approach to selling requires ideas. This is fundamental. Ideas come from everywhere. If you set aside the hours from 8:00 P.M. to 10:00 P.M. each Tuesday to dream up ideas that will upgrade your work, you won't come up with many. The ideas that have to do with your very own individual act of selling don't come that way. Remember, now, we are not referring to the marketing or merchandising ideas that others in your company normally develop to help you sell. We are referring to ideas that will influence the way you sell, the procedures you use, how you solve selling problems.

Many salesmen, not all, of course, are ready to take *personal* credit for a successful sale—they contend that the company's advertising, promotion, program, and sales helps don't deserve any of the credit. *I did it—me, the salesman—alone.* Is this right or wrong? It is right! Are you surprised that we should agree? You shouldn't be. The salesman has the right to expect his company's program and advertising help. He can and should take personal credit for the sale. If the company is well-managed, it will spend just enough on sales tools to give the sales-man a good competitive chance to establish and maintain a profitable (for the company) sales relationship with his cus-tomers. The sale depends on how well the salesman personally uses these sales tools.

On the other hand, most salesmen are *not* willing to take per-sonal responsibility for a lost sale—they contend that the com-pany's advertising, promotion, program and sales helps were not enough in this instance. Just can't win 'em all. Right or wrong? Well, this is wrong in this particular. If one customer can be won in a certain set of circumstances, and if it doesn't happen with a second customer under similar circumstances, something was the matter with how the salesman handled the interview and the events leading to it. The salesman should be expected to be ingenious enough to rearrange his selling tools to meet each customer's requirements.

The salesman who indulges himself by refusing to accept full responsibility for lost or incomplete sales is going to lose commissions and personal growth opportunity needlessly. Only by assuming this responsibility will he prepare himself for learning and applying new techniques and skills toward im-proving his performance.

We haven't strayed from our subject of awareness. In fact, we're talking about it—awareness of our own responsibilities. Productive awareness is a new technique in learning how to get better results from your selling effort. Let's see how we can sharpen our senses of awareness and how we can apply what we learn to improving our selling skills with this illustration:

There were a number of new flavorful packaged snacks mak-ing their appearance. John L. was a salesman whose line in-cluded several of these new snack products. We'll call them Snacketts. John L. liked them personally, his family and friends liked them, and they were selling well in his customers' super-markets. Everything seemed to be going perfectly—especially since his company was happy with his 10% over quota perform-ance.

However, something was bothering John L. He was aware that there were others like himself who, while watching television, would go to the kitchen during commercials and bring back a snack. He, in fact, knew this was a big part of his business with these new products. His wife told John L. that she liked the Snacketts especially for cocktails before a dinner party. They were light, didn't spoil appetites, and were simple to serve, easy and convenient.

John L. thought of those thousands of TV tubes burning in his territory night after night, and the vast amount of home entertaining week after week. Although he was beating his quota on Snacketts, it dawned on him that he was probably only selling a fraction of the potential market. How could he sell more? This could be accomplished only by getting more facings and better locations in his supermarkets, but this was very, very difficult. The grocer knows that more space for one product means less space for another, and he doesn't care about dollar trading—selling more of this product only to lose it by selling less of that one.

> *Fact:* This is a selling problem. No additional advertising on the product or promotional endeavor by the company will change this situation. Only John L.'s personal selling ingenuity can do it. Will he measure up to the challenge?

John L. observed that Snacketts were, in fact, extra sales to the housewife. She bought all of the other grocery products she had intended to buy and Snacketts were on top—a pure and simple extra sale. In addition, he learned by inquiry that the product could also be served as a staple—with soup for luncheon, or with sandwiches instead of potato chips—and this could be a heavy secondary use. So, he reasoned, if Snacketts could get more than one location plus space from the more staple items that the housewife was going to buy anyway, the supermarket would take in more dollars and increase total business.

The first thing that John L. did was to make a thumbnail

survey to back up his "awareness" of this big new potential for
him.

As he was checking his facings of the product in markets he
would ask shopping housewives these questions:

1. How do you use Snacketts—as a TV snack, for parties,
   for the children, for regular meals and lunches?
2. In addition to this location in the store, where would
   you be most likely to notice them:
   a. With soft drinks, candy, ice cream and nuts?
   b. With soups? Salad ingredients? Gourmet foods?
   c. With bread, rolls, crackers, cereals?
3. Did you have Snacketts on your list or were you in-
   tending to buy them? Did you buy them as a substitute
   for something else?

Now notice that the answers to these questions are all going
to support John L.'s contention that the store should provide
more locations and bigger facings for Snacketts. He recorded
this data on a little card with the housewife's name and the
name of the supermarket. When he had enough evidence to
make his findings impressive, he approached his most cooperative supermarket customers with a new sharp selling pitch.
He explained that here was a great new source for extra sales
and profits and asked for a two weeks' test.

John L. was certain to see his sales increase with more locations and bigger facings and here too he kept a good record
of sales results. These he used in extending his "test" operations
with his other customers. Obviously, all of his customers were
loath to reduce display at the end of two weeks in the face of
increased *extra* sales.

However, John L. was just warming to his new-found potential. He observed that small "stop and shop" 24-hour drive-in
markets were springing up around his area. These are "staple"
operations but represented a good source of "impulse" sales for
Snacketts. He made a point of stopping for a short pitch at each
of these markets explaining the good results of the supers.

In each area, in one or two of the "stop and shop" stores,

John L. would leave a sample package of Snacketts for the Coke salesman with this note:

> For the Coke Salesman—In appreciation of your company's advertising slogan, "Things go better with Coke," I'd like you personally to try Snacketts because if anything goes well with Coke they do.
>
> John L.,—Blanke Company

John L. reasoned that it didn't do any harm to have a few influential friends. The Coke salesmen were not going to sell his product but they did get into those little stores everywhere and every day.

One of John L.'s friends was a TV distributor who at the moment had a "summer special"—a case of Coke with the purchase of a TV portable. John L. convinced him he should add two packages of Snacketts to the offer and advertise "A week's supply of Snacketts and Coke *free* for enjoyable summer TV viewing." He then took the ad around to his customers to emphasize the mass market connotations for Snacketts by its association with Coke.

There were dozens of ideas that John L. employed, building one on another. All of them were originally stimulated by provoking his sense of awareness. Awareness creates problems to be solved, problems require ideas, ideas solve problems and build sales.

Reminder: Constantly view these examples for their idea value in relation to *your* situation, *your* product and *your* opportunities.

To establish how ideas and solutions to selling problems come from awareness and logical thinking about what we observe, let's go through this exercise of applying awareness to a specific problem:

> You are selling a line of well-advertised and well-accepted cosmetics slanted toward the teen-age girl. You have good distribution in drug stores. You notice that the senior and junior high school classes terminate each day at 3:30 P.M. What are your thought-processes?

Well, you might reason that teen-age girls had some free time between 3:30 and 5:30 when they had to be home. You might wonder how you could use some of that time to expose them to your products. Possibly drug stores (located conveniently near school or home) could run a special on Tuesday between 4 P.M. and 5 P.M. on your line and directed toward the girl who is already thinking of that Friday night date.

You might conclude that week-day retailer advertising on your products is more productive for you than the week-end advertising which your retailers generally give to your line.

Carry through your thinking a bit further on this subject. We'll supply the situations. You supply the creative application of ideas to meet the situation:

1. You're selling writing instruments and your wife points out that you should start making plans for the family vacation.
2. You're selling men's accessories (cuff links, tie clips, etc.), and you read an article, written by a popular young female TV and movie personality, deploring men's "casual" look in attire.
3. You're selling flashlight batteries and you hear that the stores in your principal market areas have agreed to open at 10 A.M. and stay open two extra nights each week until 10 P.M.
4. You're selling luggage, and you read that the airlines announce an attractive new lower fare for teen-age travel.

If you think the opportunities in these examples are obvious, you are right. They are intended to be obvious. But how obvious are they? Really? It's the obvious in selling that seems to be most often overlooked. With this matter of awareness, we must start with the obvious and graduate to the less obvious. We're not necessarily trying to solve specific problems, but *the relationship between events and situations in our day-to-day selling activities is actually the catalyst for new selling ideas.*

First, we must develop the faculty for recognizing which of those things which we see or hear can contribute to our selling effort.

Here are six ways toward developing your own creative ideas through awareness so that you can use your merchandising tools for greater results:

1. Listen more and talk less. Obviously, you can learn from others. Practice listening. Try not to shut your mind off while others are talking. Listening is difficult, generally because a point is made and the listener stays with it while the talker goes on to the next point. "Drifting" while listening becomes a habit and it has to be broken. When you find your mind wandering, try immediately to get back with the speaker. You won't forget the first point, possibly you have missed the second point, but you will get the third.

   If you enter—*briefly*—into the conversation it will help maintain your interest and permit better listening. You may have to force yourself to listen to dull conversation, so if you cannot in some way cut it off, take heart in the knowledge that thought-provoking ideas can come from a boring dissertation as well as a sparkling one.

   Listening to statistics, for example, can be pretty boring, especially the way some people present them. However, if you are stimulated by the first or second statistic you hear into developing a point for yourself, you can be sure other statistics will give you equal stimulation and you ought to listen for them. The best way is to take notes and do your thinking and developing later.

   If you have trouble keeping your mind on the subject of a speaker in normal conversation, you should work on your listening attentiveness. For sixty days carry a small card in your change pocket which says, "Today

I shall talk less and listen more." You are not trying to win any popularity contests but in sixty days your social relationships with your friends and business associates will seem to improve. That's all it will take to keep you in a listening mood.

From this point on it is a matter of training your mind to stay on track. Notes help considerably and a salesman should never be without a pocket secretary for ready reference and note taking. It is possible for anyone to train himself to listen more attentively.

2. Maintain a good level of interest in the things you observe and the things surrounding your everyday affairs. You can't be interested in everything you see and hear and do. Much of everyone's life is routine and uninteresting; apparently nature intended it that way. However, don't smother things that might be valuable by shutting them out deliberately, not giving them a chance.

Quite an easy way to maintain interest is to practice curiosity—be a little curious about things that might be of interest in sparking ideas. How do you do this? Ask questions:

a. Ask questions of others. Even if you have to say, "What was that again?" When something sounds like it could be worthwhile find out more about it. We will later discuss the use of questions in sales conversations as a selling device; here we use questions as a means of holding our interest in things that we might employ to create ideas. A question is a question for whatever purpose it was asked—it could serve a dozen different purposes.

One thing about a question—it holds your interest because you have to be alert for the answer. You also have to evaluate the answer. The answer may tend to lessen your interest but at least you gave the subject a second chance.

b. Ask questions of yourself. In your reading, for example, pause occasionally and ask yourself a question pertaining to the subject matter. It might only be, "I wonder if this article is getting anywhere?" or, "I wonder if I should turn the page and move on to something else?" At least you gave it a second chance.

Here too, questions you ask of yourself demand an answer. The answer will either tend to heighten the interest in a subject or diminish it. Most things you discard, and that is only natural. More things will come through as groundwork for ideas that can present you with new opportunities.

c. Question yourself or others on things you observe that might have a bearing on your business. Long ago a tire salesman, observing the convenience of gasoline service stations, made the suggestion which put these stations into the retail tire business. No doubt he asked himself this question: "These stations are convenient, people come here first when anything happens to their car. I wonder if they wouldn't be good outlets for tires?"

Questioning the things you observe will also give you an indication as to whether you should continue your interest or discard it. Suppose you represent a furniture manufacturer and you pass a magnificent new high-rise apartment building with a sign "Now Leasing." You've passed many before but this time you ask yourself, "I wonder how this could affect my business?" Further thought prompts you to check with management to get a listing of new tenants. You get in touch with a principal dealer in the area with suggestions of how he can contact these prime furniture prospects with your line. In fact, you map out a whole campaign for him to follow. Next, you extend the idea to other areas.

Now this is but one example of an observation that is translated by a question into a sales problem. The sales problem requires an answer. The answer requires ideas. Ideas make business.

3. Keep an "Ingenious Ideas" notebook. We have already recommended that a salesman never be without a pocket secretary for random notes and reminders. At various times during the week, enlarge on some of the observations you have made and impressions you have gained that have a bearing on your business and which may provide food for sound selling ideas. The book can be subdivided as follows:

   a. Competitive efforts and activity.
   b. Economic factors which could affect my orders.
   c. Cross reference magazine articles and newspaper reports.
   d. Random observances and impressions of personal business interest.
   e. Specific ideas from personal experience.

   In a later chapter there will be a complete section on personal business records. Some of the things in this section will be helpful in keeping this suggested notebook, but don't confuse the two. They serve different purposes. The "Ingenious Ideas" notebook is not a record. It is a tool for developing personal selling plans and programs to increase your business.

   Work first on the competitive section because in your everyday activity you will naturally be aware of competitive activities. Write out a brief three-part section for each subject.

   a. Explain the competitive effort or activity.
   b. Point up what problem this makes for you.
   c. Comments on ideas you may have to combat the activity or, more importantly, how you might be

able to turn the activity into an asset for you. (More on this subject as the book progresses.)

Other sections of the notebook can be organized in similar fashion except for the cross reference section. You will use this notebook and, if you start it right now, you will find plenty of subject matter as you proceed with this book.

4. Draw on the experience of others. There is no purpose in making mistakes others have already made if you can avoid it. At the same time, you can build ingenious sales ideas by improving on the techniques of other salesmen in your field and outside.

Learn to ask pointed questions of salesmen in other fields that you meet in waiting rooms, coffee shops, hotel lobbies. These are not usually conversations anyway, but a few brief comments. If you can make them profitable to you, so much the better.

Keep your ears open and mouth shut at your own sales meetings. Get all the ideas you can about how others are doing specific jobs. Use your "Ingenious Ideas" notebook. If wholesalers or manufacturers' representatives handle your line for you, lean heavily on their salesmen. Get to know them and draw them out on your merchandise. They will find plenty of problems, and ideas come from problems. In addition, you will get help in what to emphasize and what not to mention in the sales meetings you conduct for them.

Trade magazines in your selling field are excellent sources of information on your dealers' activities and their business information. These publications lean heavily on idea testimonials and experience. In the stationery field these publications include: *Office Appliances, Modern Stationer, Geyers Topics, National Stationer* and others, including regional books. Drug magazines include *Drug Topics, American Druggist, Drug Trade News, Chain Store Drug Age* and others.

Jewelry publishers are: *Jewelers National Keystone, National Jeweler, Modern Jeweler* and others, plus regional magazines. These are but a few of the areas and publications printed.

5. Draw on your own experiences. Covering the whole subject of "awareness," this could be the most idea-provoking area of all. Many salesmen do not make good idea use of their own experiences principally because, as we have previously mentioned, they fail to accept the responsibility for lost sales. How do you excuse the lost sale?

   a. Do you simply walk away from it without a second thought and move on to the next sale?
   b. Do you give it some thought and end up by saying that it was the fault of advertising, program, promotion, or point-of-sale policies?
   c. Did the customer tell you that your proposition just doesn't fit his situation?
   d. Do you honestly try to review the interview to discover either what you did or didn't do that influenced the negative decision?

   You must accept responsibility for the lost sale. Then you must review the lost sale and pinpoint the reasons for it. On the surface it will always seem to be the fault of advertising, promotion, or point-of-sale policies, or that your offer just doesn't fit. You must dig deeper and ask, "Why not? Why did it work for dealer A and not for dealer B?" The answer is always that you didn't make it work.

   Now it's easy to accept the credit for a successful sale. But here again, to create ingenious selling techniques by drawing on experience, you must determine why the sale was successful.

   a. Do you walk away from a successful sale with a good feeling and an empty head?

b. Do you credit it to the advertising program by saying, "This time the program really worked"?
c. Did the customer take the offer away from you to the extent that no real selling was involved?
d. Do you try to review the interview to discover either what you did or didn't do that influenced the successful decision?

How do you make your experience pay off for you? As you make out your daily report each evening, mentally review each call. Ask yourself, "What did I do right?—wrong? What selling points seemed strongest?—weakest? Where was the turning point in the sale? Was there anything unusual about this sale?" These are types of questions—there are others. If there are particularly important points that you want to remember, make a note for your "Ingenious Ideas" notebook.

Experience is a great teacher, but you must make it work as a teacher by analyzing and reviewing and applying what it teaches.

6. Try to keep yourself from becoming a victim of habit. You do have to develop routine to be efficient, but the canned sales talk can become a way of life. It doesn't meet all selling situations and resists change to a better procedure. All of us develop a "canned" selling pitch to a degree and it is desirable to do so. Actually, the more "routine" we get, however, the less ingenious we become. There need not be a conflict if we review our selling calls as recommended above and alter our presentations accordingly.

Examine all of your routine patterns to determine if there isn't a better way. Drive to the market a different way next time. Shave on the left side of your face first instead of the right. Brush your teeth after you shave rather than before. In other words, don't interrupt your routine, just change it around a bit. Determine for yourself just how many little things you have put yourself into the habit of doing. Ideas and invention fight habit.

When you drive around your territory, vary the streets and roads from time to time. You might notice accounts you are missing. Where taking inventory is a problem, try writing ahead to see if a sales person can take the inventory for you before you arrive. Where the buyer is "prepared" to give you a "no" because of a long standing appointment, try an unannounced call on important selling news.

The creative person always attempts to stay out of the rut—he circumvents routine by seeking a better way. You really can't avoid habit or eliminate routine but you can minimize its effect upon your creativity.

This chapter has provoked your thinking on the subjects of change and awareness and their importance in getting the ideas that effect improvements in our total selling procedures. We've discussed the reasons why your individual selling tactics, the various ways which you are now using in actually conducting your selling job, i.e., your level of *awareness,* should be open to question.

There's an old saying, "You can't improve on success." In the stock market it goes, "You can't make a mistake taking a profit." This is plain rubbish and a salve for inefficiency and error.

1. The facts are you must improve on success. Anything less, is, in reality, failure. If our only changes were based on failure, we'd still be chipping rocks in the stone ages. The trouble is determining what success really is. The salesman is often hesitant to even think about change. He associates it with experimentation, and he feels he is beyond that.

    Fortunately, you can't go backward in knowledge, so far as techniques and skills are concerned. You simply discard the poor and improve on the good. The only way you can go is up.

2. It isn't a matter of redoing all you are doing and starting all over again. Far from it. As new ways and means work their way into organizing your work, routing, planning your time, conducting your sales interviews, you inject these new elements into your procedures one by one, bit by bit. Get away from the conception that the only things that can help you are more advertising, a different consumer free offer, more discounts for your customer, better and more costly displays and dispensers, easier credit terms and all the other considerations that your company has to give to you.

   Concentrate your thinking and ideas as much as possible on what you can do to use the tools you have more effectively. The feelings of power and accomplishment which you obtain when you use the same tools as others, but with greater results, is the competitive aspect of selling that makes it the enjoyable and enriching profession that it is.

Thus, the first of the learning techniques in discovering a new, different and more productive way to sell is to apply awareness in a way that adds more profitable results from our daily effort. You will learn, as we proceed further, just how to use this technique advantageously. Now, let's investigate additional learning techniques, first in the form of an inventory of your natural talents.

4

Taking Inventory of Your Natural Talents for Ingenious Selling— Confidence, Attitude And Individual Organization

Let's explore a most fascinating subject—ourselves. Let's find some talents we didn't know we had and learn how to use them. Let's even examine some attributes we know we will never possess in full measure, but of which we can still make some use. And by all means, let's make our assets do double duty for us.

Now all of this sounds like a big order, and it would be, excepting that each of us is stronger than we think, especially when we can make our weak points work for us as well as our strong points. This is why a "standpat" sales training course just doesn't work for everybody. You will never see any two outstanding salesmen who operate in the same manner. The only thing they have in common is a top level selling performance.

Certainly, one good salesman can always learn from another, but what he learns he adapts to his own techniques in his own way. Every sales situation is different from every other, even to the extent of calls on the same customer. Yet there is a pattern, albeit a slight one, and we can keep a semblance of order by using this pattern as a pathway for our discussion.

Our first approach is to spend time thinking about ourselves and as this is an individual matter it will be permissible to let our thoughts wander off now and then as we move along. Fact is, we shall try to provoke just that. And keep in mind that our basic concern in this chapter is the *inventory* of our natural talents. Here are the important personal inventory items:

Item No. 1—How is my confidence ratio? Do I have an image with my social and working associates as a confident person? Confidence is a key factor to immediate selling successes and the total growth pattern.

Item No. 2—What are my attitudes toward my day-to-day assignments, my company people, products and programs? Attitudes have a strong bearing on successful sales interviews.

Item No. 3—How do I plan and organize my time? Really, how well organized am I generally, at leisure as well as at work? There are secrets to becoming better organized.

It's now time to begin the inventory count. A logical sequence, it would seem, would be to start with Item No. 1.

The Confidence Factor

How much confidence do you have in yourself? In your native ability? In your company, its goals and ambitions, its working tools and programs? Do you consider yourself a decision-maker?

Confidence is a broadly used term and in its broadest sense it is an attribute that every individual in selling must possess in order to enjoy the fruits of success in his chosen profession. But confidence can be acquired—absolutely. In fact, 99 per cent of it *is* acquired. Some people have the capacity to acquire it more quickly than others and in greater quantities. Some others may acquire it in such quantities that they become overconfident and even overbearing.

Let's do a bit of confidence measuring. Here's a "for instance."

Your office has left word that the president of a good prospect company is staying at a hotel in your headquarters city and you are to contact him. You are unable to get further instructions or information. Check yourself on the following:

1. I would telephone for an appointment:
    a. If refused, would breathe a sigh of relief that it wasn't really my problem anyway.
    b. If refused, would make another valiant attempt to make an appointment somehow.
    c. If accepted, would really have felt more comfortable about the whole thing if it had been refused.
    d. If accepted, would look forward to the unknown interview as an opportunity and challenge.
2. I would call for the appointment from the lobby of the hotel where I would be immediately available.
3. I would steer clear of the whole situation because with so few facts I could do more harm than good.

Now, suppose a luncheon meeting were arranged:

A. I would "bone up" on my program and make some definite plans for the interview.
B. I would feel that not knowing the situation, the best procedure would be to "be myself" and play it by ear.

Actually, there are no rights or wrongs here—this is an exercise in a measure of confidence. If you checked 1(a), you are dependable but not very confident. If you checked 1(c), you'll be glad to know that apprehension has nothing to do with confidence. You may never feel comfortable about an interview but that doesn't mean you can't make it come off.

If you checked (2), you were showing adroitness rather than confidence. If you checked (3), you may have a confidence problem—even if you held your opinion in all honesty. If you checked B, you are loaded with confidence, but checking A doesn't mean you don't have it.

Confidence is as necessary to the salesman as rain to the grass. The salesman must take command of every selling situation and has to be absolutely sure of himself to do it. He must make an advance decision about his routing plans and then stick with it. That requires confidence. He must make a decisional plan for each call and then work his plan—that, too, requires confidence.

You won't acquire all the confidence you need by knowing all the facts and details of the proposition you are selling—but it sure helps.

You won't obtain all the confidence you need to do a better job by learning new techniques via this book and in other ways —but that helps, too.

You get confidence by being right—and knowing it. This is the "certain" method of increasing your confidence ratio. You must believe in what you are doing and how you are doing it. *You must believe that what you tell the retailer and the wholesaler is the gospel truth. If he does what you tell him, what you tell him will come true.* If you believe anything less than that, you risk a confidence waver and if a buyer senses it you've lost a sale.

That's why confidence is so important—its effect upon the customer. He must know that you believe without question that your offer is right for him. Your own confidence has to shine through. Now, regardless of your sales success you should explore this confidence factor in your own selling effort. Try this suggestion:

Take a certain part of your current program that you have some doubts about. Tell yourself simply that you are wrong to have those doubts. Recall the positive things discussed about this specific proposition at your last sales meeting and list them. Dig out any bulletins or written material and jot down a few notes. Now, organize the strongest sales pitch you can muster.

Pick out ten prospects for this special effort and route yourself to reach them within a reasonable time. Give the whole effort the real college try—and, remember, you must absolutely believe—no foolin'.

Here's advance notice of what will happen—just exactly what you predict to your customer in your sales interview! Why? Because you'll make it happen. You will be so positive that the buyer will believe, too; and if he believes he'll make it happen. This is why the impossible often becomes the possible.

Now, all of this is a full time project, and while you might classify it as an exercise in measuring your confidence factor, it obviously can turn out to be a very valuable lesson on an earn-as-you-learn basis. In this chapter we are merely taking an inventory of ourselves—measuring our capacities. It's always desirable to devise a means to do this that pays a profit.

If you intend to use this suggestion to measure your confidence factor, you should mark your place and make a few notes.

1. List a product or offer that you have not been successful with and that you have doubts about.
2. List all the positive things you can as picked up at sales meetings, in bulletins, and convince yourself that you have been wrong—sell yourself.
3. Develop a strong sales presentation and a means for introducing it into your general presentation.
4. List the ten prospects—and they must be logical candidates for the offer—that you can incorporate in your current routing.
5. Work the plan—and after you have seen all ten prospects determine whether you have a better measure on what a more confident approach can do for your whole selling effort.

Now, we can generalize by identifying these three ways to measure and improve your confidence factors:

1. Learn all about your products, their features, consumer benefits, retailer and wholesaler benefits, so that you can answer any questions about them. Feel that you have an answer for any question.
2. Ditto your advertising, displays, point-of-sale material, promotions, offers, program. Have all the answers, maybe not always a hundred per cent right answer but an answer nevertheless.

3. Rehearse your sales presentation—determine what you're going to say and how you are going to say it and predict the results for your customer. This is imperative. "Mr. Dealer, if you do this and this and this, your results will be these." Only predict for your customer what you yourself can believe—and you must believe it.

And a few more: Believe in yourself. If you are not organized as well as you would like to be, keep working on it and work for the day when you *will* be better organized. Dress and keep your appearance so that the buyer will remember what you say and not how you look. Lick any bad mannerisms that you know you have. It will take resolve to do this. Take reasonable care of your health. There's nothing that will buoy confidence like feeling well. Embrace a reasonably optimistic outlook and a pleasant demeanor.

The Attitude Factor

Confidence is catching. In a way, it's really what you're selling as well as what your customer is buying. But now let's move along to another most important subject, that of inventorying and analyzing your attitudes. Analyze a few case histories:

John L. is a good salesman with a successful sales record, but his daily results would be better and his growth prospects brighter with a better attitude. John is a compulsive complainer. He does a good job but in his eyes it is a fantastic job considering the obstacles and handicaps he works under. Eighty per cent of his job, he believes, is devoted to correcting the horrendous mistakes of others—only twenty per cent is selling. The program only works in the way that he puts it together; and if he goes on record that something is wrong or things won't work, he'll go to any length to prove it.

John L. is carefully supervised. He has been told these things about himself but he secretly doesn't believe them. Because John L. is understood and closely watched, his excellent sales attributes are brought to the fore and his performance is good.

But if John L. is ever put adrift, he will be lost. He just wouldn't be able to understand why he actually is on constant probation with his company.

But fortunately, John L.'s attitude problem is curable if he will admit honestly to himself the problem and diligently follow a few simple steps to cleanse his warped attitude. First, he must convince himself that his company could get along without him. Second, he should practice listening carefully at sales meetings, both to the sales presentations and to other salesmen. Third, he should accept each program at its face value and develop his sales procedures around it. He will find complaints but they will be genuine and not invented.

William P. is also a good salesman with a successful sales record, but his daily results would be better and his growth prospects brighter with a better attitude. William P. is a gloomy-gus pessimist. If his company puts on a special drive for business, his first reaction is, "How are we going to do it with the weak program we have to work with and the obvious strength of our competitor's?" He predicts dire failure and he has the reasons for it well catalogued.

William P. also must be closely supervised. He must be "sold" over and over again on his own strengths and his program's strengths. He recognizes that he makes a "critical" appraisal of his job assignment and the tools he has to work with, but he doesn't recognize this as downright pessimism. He is always three days behind before he can be sold that the job can be accomplished.

William P. can never take a positive approach to solving his own problems with this pessimistic attitude. He will always need help, although he has almost all of the capabilities of carving out a successful career save one—attitude. William P. can almost always do what he sets out to do and his performance is good, but only because his supervisor understands him and values his worth. If that relationship were changed a dangerous situation could develop for William P.

Here, too, we have an attitude problem that is curable, but

only if the supervisor and William P. work on the real problem and try to solve it rather than attempt to simply understand it and to work with it or around it.

Charles C. is a knitpicker. He never reviews a program to determine how he can best present it. Rather, he tries to find out where the i's are not dotted and the t's are not crossed. He delights in bringing his findings to light and making some clerk in the home office look stupid. He would be happier as a proofreader.

Carl W. is a supervisor criticizer. He never gets the word and always writes the general sales manager about it. He feels he's making time for himself but the G.S.M. interprets it as excuse for poor performance. Other men under the same supervisor seem to get the word. He should be writing the movie reviews for his hometown newspaper.

George D. is a program replanner. He's the kind of fellow who follows the marketing director out of the sales meeting with this lead-off remark: "Charlie, do you know what we need—?" He reviews the program with an eye to changing it so it will work for him. If George D. were really creative, he would make better use of what he has and use the proper time and place to make what would be welcomed suggestions.

Walt S. is an exception finder. With him the exception is the rule. He makes a sale that is out of line and he'll find the omission or misstatement in the program to justify it. If he is granted an exception for one of his accounts, he will immediately apply it to other accounts—or insist that it be allowed. He should be reading briefs in an attorney's office.

That's enough of the case histories for the moment anyway. All we wish to accomplish here is to establish a base for determining our own attitudes, and take an attitude inventory, as it were.

Your own attitude toward your job, your company, your company's management and your customers has great bearing on your past, present and future results. There probably isn't such a thing as a definable attitude. It's too personal. But your basic attitudes, if you analyze them and find them wanting, can be changed—not as readily as opinions, but changed nevertheless. Remember first these guidelines.

In the areas of human relations—which includes selling—the image of yourself that you reveal to others is paramount. It isn't who you are but who others think you are, and every one of your acquaintances knows you as someone a little different. It isn't what you say, but what others hear. It isn't what you do, but what others believe you do. Does this mean you should attempt to rearrange your personality to fit a pattern? Absolutely not. These truisms simply make it possible for you to establish the kind of image you want. They are useful tools available for your use. Exploiting these truisms is the way to make your attitudes pay big dividends in immediate selling results and long term personal growth.

Take this simple test:

1. One of the top marketing people shows up unexpectedly and announces that he would like to make a couple of calls with you. Check one of the closest to what you think your attitude would be:
   (a) You look on the situation as an opportunity to demonstrate your qualities in a good light.
   (b) You wonder why he really came, and you resent a little not having enough facts.
   (c) You consider it an imposition as you have your work planned and the interruption will only slow you down.

If you thought about it and answered with complete honesty, and if you checked (c), you resent authority. Almost everybody does. How do you like to be stopped by a policeman? Your problem is that you are too obvious—you'll have to do something about the attitude itself to control it better.

If you checked (b), you have the attitude under a little better control. But you still have to be careful.

If you checked (a), you have the attitude of resentment against authority well under control. In fact, you are using your attitude to good advantage.

Review the above comments carefully. Are they realistic? Do they really add up to common sense? Do they convince *YOU?*

What attitudes can your company reasonably expect of you:

1. That you will "follow the company line" in all your endeavors and not vary except with permission. This rule should apply at every executive level.
2. That you will request exceptions to the rule only after making an honest effort to comply with company policy.
3. If your point of view does not prevail, you will accept the company decision in good grace.
4. Because the salesman is a problem solver and decision maker, the company may reasonably expect that company interests come before customer or personal interests.

This latter requirement is somewhat difficult at times because it often appears to the salesman that it is the customer who really makes out his pay check. Not true—the salesman is really paid out of profits and not sales. Loyalty always is first to the company.

Now you should give some separate thought to your attitudes toward your company, its policies, people, and programs; your customers, your assigned duties, the disagreeable aspects of your job. Are your attitudes objective and positive? If not, you must make one of two choices—correct them or make a change.

Attitudes are relatively easy to correct unless too deep-seated. The way to do it is to be conscious of your thinking—from an attitude standpoint. Let's illustrate from a situation: You receive an upsetting letter from headquarters.

Your first reaction is anger. They have their nerve sending through a letter like that! The next reaction is hurt. How could they do this to me? The third reaction is concern. How do I get out of this situation? Then analysis begins—to marshal the facts for an answer.

Stop! Can you now assume an objective and positive attitude? Did you deserve the letter, really, or is it simply a misunderstanding? Can you put yourself in the letter-writer's shoes and understand his point of view?

You can inventory your attitudes as a part of this exercise, and possibly hit them pretty close. But your real test is to determine your attitudes under fire and on a day-to-day, situation-to-situation basis. If you can stop and say, "I'd better think this one over and determine what my attitude should be," you've got it made.

You cannot have a successful selling day if your attitudes are awry. Your customers will interpret it as insincerity. You will not be alert and perceptive. You will get smaller orders; you will lose orders.

Whenever the day doesn't seem to be going right, ask yourself: "Is there something bugging me today? I can't sell unless I believe in what I am doing and how I'm doing it. Better get my attitudes straightened out—right now. I'll give the whole subject some thought this evening, after the stores close." If you can do that you won't have a problem tonight; you'll already have solved it. You'll have recovered from a disease which you can label "attituditis."

The Organization Factor

Well, now, let's inventory some of the more specific attributes and natural talents that lend themselves to successful immediate and long-term sales results The first of these is personal organization. How well organized are you for your immediate assignment? We shall discuss organization for personal growth in another chapter.

One of the old saws in selling has been: "The more time you keep yourself in front of buyers the better sales results you will have." While one wouldn't want to dispute the law of averages, this philosophy may not be the only answer for many salesmen.

One obvious exception is the sales interview that requires exacting and detailed preparation: facts and figures, charts and graphs, hours of extensive research and study. Stepping out of consumer goods selling for the moment, a drastic example would be the road-building machinery salesman. There are few buyers, an interview might take a week, preparation several months.

But back to consumer products. Generally, preparation is an "after hours" proposition, and being in front of buyers during store open hours is certainly important. None the less, in your inventory of organization of your time, there are other factors to keep in mind. Number one is that in today's economy the consumer is King. Today (and the trend is growing) the consumer has a great choice of products and brands of the same product types. Point-of-sale display in drug, department, stationery and jewelry stores is very important—facings in supermarkets and discount outlets. Not only getting the display but keeping the display up and keeping it stocked in your absence is paramount.

So, in organizing your time, it might be well to know the amount of time you must (not should) spend in insuring that your product has the best chance for sale. If this requires daylight hours for such things as picking up material at warehouses, freight depots and express offices, or telephone appointments with store and outside display people, your time organization becomes more complex.

The best method is to stop-watch yourself through a few days. A schedule might run as follows:

8:00 A.M.—Left hotel

8:25 A.M.—Arrived express office—(duty)

9:05 A.M.—Store (1) (display and inventory)

9:25 A.M.—   "   (merchandise manager and buyer)

9:40 A.M.—   "   (coffee)

9:55 A.M.—   "   (worked with buyer)

10:15 A.M.—   "   (settled on order—write out details to-night)

10.25 A.M.—   "   (talked to counter people)

10.40 A.M.—   "   (left store—order amount $_____)

That call has consumed two hours and forty minutes.

10.50 A.M.—Store (2) (display and inventory)
11:00 A.M.—   "   (worked with buyer—wrote order)
11:15 A.M.—   "   (left store—order $_____)

Call time: thirty-five minutes (from leaving last store).

11:20 A.M.—Telephone appointments
11:40 A.M.—Store (3) (display and inventory)
11:55 A.M.—   "   (ready to see buyer—out to lunch)
12:15 P.M.—Lunch
12:55 P.M.—Store (4) (display and inventory)
 1:10 P.M.—   "   (see buyer—no order)
 1:20 P.M.—Store (3) (see buyer—write order $_____)

Two calls—two hours and five minutes (from leaving last store).

 2:05 P.M.—Wholesaler (1) (go over inventory with buyer)
 2:30 P.M.—   "   (work with sales manager)
 2:50 P.M.—   "   (write up order $_____)
 3:20 P.M.—   "   (bulletin/sales meeting details)

Call time—two hours (from leaving last store).

 3:40 P.M.—Store (5) (display and inventory)
 4:00 P.M.—   "   (left store—call back)
 4:15 P.M.—Store (6) (display and inventory)
 4:30 P.M.—   "   (see buyer $_____ order)
 4:50 P.M.—   "   (talked to counter people)
 5:35 P.M.—Returned to hotel

Call time—two calls—two hours and fifteen minutes (from leaving wholesaler).

 6:40 P.M.—Completed daily reports and order writing.

Results: Seven calls—five orders—$_____.

Your day may be vastly different from this example. Possibly you have much daytime driving. Or, you may have "preliminary to call" requirements for using some of those important 8 A.M.–5 P.M. hours. You might be able to utilize evening hours —and this would be a part of your organization inventory.

In any event, the key to becoming better organized, or we should put it, more efficient, with a greater daily return, is to keep a time schedule—periodically. You may want to do this on a daily basis, that is a day or two now and then, or you may want to keep a strict schedule over a week or two. In the latter case, you might record a week in and a week out of your headquarters city.

Next, you will want to determine what you do during the day that is the most productive for you.

1. Is it time in front of the buyer, making the sales presentation and getting agreement on an order and the amount of the order?
2. Is it time with merchandise managers, display, and advertising people, planning store promotion with your products?
3. Is it display positioning, inventorying, replacing or updating, servicing the account?
4. Is it accumulating data in regard to your products, competitors' products, related products and other elements that will help you to get better cooperation, position and sales in any particular store?

Obviously, the more orders you write and the bigger they are the better off you are—unless:

a. You can't go back for a reorder.
b. The merchandise doesn't move.
c. You leave the account with unanswered complaints.
d. Even though you got an order your call left your competitor better off than you.

Now, there are two great dangers to good personal organization—watch out for them:

1. Changing your mind after your plans have been made. Rarely should you do it. You can't be organized without a plan, and the plan isn't worth much unless it's followed.
2. Setting a "comfortable" working level. For example, planning an easy daily schedule of calls, or a very safe weekly routing. When you set a comfortable schedule you invite wasted time and inefficiency.

We shall examine good routing and planning in subsequent chapters. Now, however, as you inventory your organizational ability you cannot help but do a little self-examination at the same time. These are but keys to take an accurate account of your organizational attributes, and no matter how good they are there are ways to make them more productive. In addition to daily work routing and planning, you have additional questions to ask of yourself:

1. Do I handle my day's detail each day so that it doesn't accumulate?
2. Does my "system" of accounting seem cumbersome and time-consuming?
3. Do I find myself using personal time such as weekends "catching up"?
4. How well organized is my personal or leisure time? Do I find myself "too tired" or "disinclined" to do odd jobs about the house or to enjoy a Sunday afternoon outing with the family?
5. Do I devote some time each week to selective reading? And to a well-liked hobby?

A salesman who is well organized both in a personal and business sense will make twice the progress, twice as fast, as one who is not well organized. Don't let yourself think you are a good self-organizer if you are not. This does happen.

People often think they are someone they are not. Think of people you know. Do you know a person who thinks he is a great judge of character—but you know he is not? Ladies man? News analyst? Intellectual? Story-teller?

Take a good impersonal inventory count on your own organizational ability. It's important to you. Of all the natural talents, organization is the one that you can do the most about. In fact, the subject of personal organization will be examined in more detail in the following chapter.

5

How to Acquire and Employ Good Organizational Habits For More Successful Selling Results

Ingeniousness in selling begins with personal organization. In this chapter we will organize and plan. We will establish the standards for organization that produce results. We will map our strategy, as in a military sense, with a result in mind.

Organization Begins with the End

It may appear at the moment that we are looking mighty far into the future in organizing and planning for our immediate selling tasks. However, really good organization requires this kind of analysis. So, let's scrutinize end goals and objectives first.

A well-planned lifetime of selling should naturally have as its objectives:

1. Above-average retirement income for leisure enjoyment and travel following your working years.
2. Above-average life insurance and current estate values to provide for your family if something should happen to you.
3. Above-average disability and health programs if either poor health or an accident should interrupt your work.

4. Above-average current income so that you can live well and plan for such things as your children's education and still enjoy an increasingly improved standard of living.

Many of these considerations are, as a rule, partially available in company "fringe benefit" plans. You should study your company's plan thoroughly, project it years ahead and, taking into account social security on the one hand and inflation on the other, determine what you will have to do to attain your immediate and future financial goals. This is not an easy exercise, what with a changing tax picture, for example, and a growing family. Nevertheless, it represents a task that must be done to properly organize for today's duties. Now you could determine, before you go far in this analysis, that you are with the wrong company for attaining your projected goals. Even if this is the case, you will still want to consider how you organize yourself today for your growth opportunities tomorrow.

Let's work from a simple formula. Suppose you are 35 years old, married 10 years with a family of three. You have a $30,000 house with a $20,000 mortgage and your *take home earnings* (after taxes, insurance, social security, etc.) approximate $10,000 per year. At age 65 you figure social security will pay you $150 per month and your wife will get $75, or a total of $225. The mortgage will be paid off, the children educated, and you will need $800 a month, $9,600 a year (not including taxes) to live as expected.

Your company plan will pick up $350 per month, your social security $150 (forget your wife's social security contribution), which totals $500—you are going to need $300 monthly or $72,000 savings at five per cent interest. If your present savings are $12,000 you must save (actually accumulate) $2,000 a year average. You can't do it on present income, but what about future possibilities? Make a plan chart. Use the following format but note, however, that this is not a complete thirty-year example but only a roughed-in form to illustrate a method of developing a personal projection.

Age	Year	After Tax Income Expected	Unusual Expenses	Interest & Savings	Accumu-lation
35	1968	$10,000	—	$ 600	$12,600
36	1969	$10,500	—	$ 900	$13,500
37	1970	$11,000	—	$1,000	$14,500
44	1977	$12,500	$2,000	—	$20,000
46	1979	$12,500	$4,000	—	$18,000
48	1981	$15,000	$4,000	—	$22,000
52	1985	$15,000	—	$2,500	$35,000
65	1998	$20,000	—	$5,000	$72,000

Now, if your progress is slow, steady and certain as in the above program, you will just make your goals. But you can't depend on it at all. The trouble is you are just skating by right now at your income level and some good breaks along the way have enabled you to accumulate the first $12,000. You need to:

1. Raise your after-tax income to $12,500 immediately on the potential you have.
2. Prove to your company you can assume more responsibility (more potential) to a $15,000 net income.
3. Broaden your perspective to becoming a supervisor to also earn off the potential of others to $18,000 income.
4. Go on from these—and with these objectives plan a new chart.

Once you do this you have an overall objective for your organization down to planning each individual call. And, because you have a specific overall objective, the manner in which you conduct yourself will take on new meaning. For example, a customer call may be viewed not entirely as an effort to get the largest order possible this trip but, instead, to building the customer to bigger and better repeat orders—to grow with the customer. His success becomes your success.

On the other hand, you may view your territory as but a stepping stone to a territory change and/or a supervisory or marketing assignment. Growth of the territory in this instance becomes less important to you (it is always important to your company) than immediate wide distribution of your products in inventory depth. The retailer will feature and sell that which he has most of. He will repeat on the lines that sell and make money. You may reason that to gain your goals you must exploit your present opportunities.

At this juncture, we are examining how best to plan to attain our overall objectives. Let's liken it to a vacation trip. The overall objectives might be to effect a change—get some mental rest—have a good time—heighten your zest for getting back on the job. With a two weeks' vacation it is quite possible that a 6,000 mile automobile camping trip with the children just may not attain these vacation objectives.

The first step, then, in organizing is to anticipate the end result. We have determined what we want the end results to be—and quite specifically. We now return to the present to begin our broad planning to attain our objective. This we do with a simple outline. Here's an example:

1. My present territory produces $100,000 a year on which my total income is ten per cent, or $10,000. I get $4,000 a year for travel. My goal for the next three years is to get this figure up to $135,000 with a resulting income of $13,500. I must concentrate on growth for my present customers plus some new account distribution. I must weed out the deadwood and replace it with livelier and more productive accounts.
2. At the end of three years I want the company to realize my worth by giving me the opportunity to build in another area with more potential which will result in an increase in income.
3. At the end of five years I want to be a district supervisor with a further increase in income as a result of my efforts in building extra volume through others.
4. At the end of ten years I want to have earned the right to assume the duties of a regional manager with both

administrative and supervisional duties—and with another boost in income.

5. I see myself eventually as a top sales, marketing or merchandising executive, and when I attain that level I will be prepared in experience and know-how, to be a success in that capacity.

Your general outline may not coincide with this at all. It may be more modest in its ambitions, or more aggressive. In any event, always remember that it is better to be ten pounds overweight in your current job than one ounce too light in the next. So now, this is the very first step in good organization. Anticipate the end result and set your course to realize your ambitions. All of your organizational efforts will benefit from this broad perspective of future goals. Take the time to outline your long range goals with a tentative timetable. After you have read this chapter return to it and develop an "income-growth" chart to age 65.

Elements of Good Organization

There are two major elements to good planning and organization for more effective selling. They are knowledge and *applied* experience.

A. You must know your products or services; i.e., the things you are selling, thoroughly. You must know their good features and their negative features. You must know your products from a consumer's "use" standpoint, from a retailer's "turnover and profit" standpoint, and from a wholesaler's storage, credit and "sell through" standpoint.

How much do you know about the things you sell? Get a pad and pen and list your products and product features right now. Indicate what you consider product weaknesses and list these, too. Now pick a product and answer this question aloud for yourself: As a consumer why would I buy this product? What are the CONSUMER benefits—not just features—but benefits?

For example:

Suppose your whidget is made of stainless steel—this is the major feature. The consumer benefit (why he would buy) would be *less corrosion* and *longer wear*. Suppose the slacks you sell are crease-resistant. Sure, they look better longer but the real consumer benefit is the *convenience* of not having to send them out to be pressed.

So, what are we trying to accomplish? We are organizing our thinking about our products and putting our knowledge about them into usable form. We have started with the consumer and we must have knowledge of him so that we can determine his reaction to the benefits of our products and how he can be sold.

Now let's examine what we have to sell from the RETAILER's bird's-eye view. He wants to know how your whidget will sell and how much profit he will make. He is thinking about repeat business and customer satisfaction. He wants to know how to display the whidget for greater sales and possibly how he can advertise it over his store's name.

Here we organize our thinking in another way about our product—how it is packaged and promoted and sold to the retailer. Again we are putting knowledge together in usable form —and this is all a part of getting properly organized.

The WHOLESALER's viewpoint is a third consideration. He wants to know how fast he can expect retailer repeat orders. Can his salesmen carry whidget samples conveniently? Are there storage and warehouse handling problems? Will he be required to give his accounts extended credit? What incentives are there for his retailer to buy? Are there P.M.'s as extra income to encourage his men to sell?

Again we look at the product and program, this time through the wholesaler's eyes and list answers to all these questions. Then we organize our thinking on both our product and his policies in the light of interest to the wholesaler. We ask ourselves why would the wholesaler buy and sell this product?

Sure, profit and turnover enter in, but so do convenience, product consumer demand, brand prestige.

To review a bit: Certainly a prerequisite of good planning and organizing one's self is product knowledge, packaging knowledge, program knowledge. Once we have this knowledge catalogued, we then proceed to think like a consumer, think like a retailer, and think like a wholesaler. We are now beginning to get properly organized. We are beginning to think of the whole selling function in an organized way. Later we will put all these things together and organize not only the interview but the events leading to it and procedures following it. First, there are some other applications of the element knowledge:

   B. You must know your own customers and your markets. Organizing your routing schedules and planning your time are, of course, paramount. You can't do it properly without intimate knowledge of your customers and the markets in which you and they operate.

First some general comments:

   a. If you sell drug stores, for example, how much do you know about the drug business? How does your product line fit in with the typical retail drug operation? How is the turnover and profit of your products measured against some other kinds of products the druggist sells? What is your time worth to the druggist? Do you know enough about his fountain business, prescription business, sundries business, to be conversive?
   b. The same technique should be examined in stationery, department, jewelry stores, restaurants, country clubs, bars, banks, industrial accounts, garages—anyone you may sell. Obtain a current trade publication in any of these retail operations and read it through to be up on current conversational topics. Know enough about these business customers to be able to discuss subjects surrounding their business other than your own product interests.

Now make a checklist of your own principal customer trade classifications. In each classification ask yourself a few simple questions such as:

1. What is the principal profit revenue department in this trade classification?
2. What would be considered an average profit for an average operation?
3. What would be considered average gross sales for an average operation?
4. What brand product names are essential for the successful operation of this business?
5. What is my line's relationship to the profit and sales of an average operation?

You can ask yourself any additional questions that are pertinent and finally you say to yourself: What else of importance do I know about this trade classification?

Now you are fitting things into place; organizing knowledge into usable form. This is an essential step into getting yourself organized for more productive selling.

C. Now let's get quite specific. How well do you know your territory? Do you know highways, directions, out-of-the-way markets, streets and locations in cities and towns, parking locations? Have you checked lately for new shopping areas or stores you haven't visited? Do you know the accounts where your principal competitor is strong? How do they compare with your strength accounts?

Good routing requires that you allow the proper time in each market to exploit *that market on that trip*. Knowledge of the market itself is essential for proper routing. It is usually not feasible to completely cover each market on each visit. It is, however, possible to obtain a maximum amount of business on each visit by properly allocating your time to the most profitable opportunities of each routing occasion. We will return to routing after we have explored further the basic elements required for good organization.

Knowledge, we have said, is the first prerequisite to good personal planning and organization. We talked about product and program knowledge. This is largely a matter of study and memorization. Next we discussed trade classification knowledge, and then territorial knowledge. This is primarily a result of experience.

D. The fourth area of knowledge required for good personal organization is a knowledge of your own opportunity. This is a result of awareness which was examined in an earlier chapter. If you don't know what you are reaching for, you will have a difficult time getting properly organized to get it. Opportunity is quite simply the various kinds of openings available to you to get more business than you are now getting. It may take many forms:

a. Retail counters where your product is not but should be on display.

b. Stores where your merchandise is so shallow in consumer selection that you lose sales.

c. The majority of your customers could do more business on your line but they haven't been sold. Your presentation is weak.

d. Loopholes in your competitor's operation or in his program as well as weak competitor representation in your area.

Very possibly you can add even more ideas of opportunity for you in your territory. Give this matter some thought right now and list the things that mean more sales potential.

How can you do more business? Try using the different "if" approach: *If* I could only find time to get to my fringe area accounts, and suburban accounts more often. I must organize my time to do this. *If* I could get the retail clerks to get my product into the act on 50 per cent more consumer inquiries. I must organize my effort to do this. *If* I could just make two

more effective calls each day. I must organize my routing schedule to do this.

Notice we don't say, "If I had more advertising" or, "If I
had a different display" or, "If my competitor would drop dead"
or, "If I had a new product." Sure, these things do represent
opportunity, but they do not represent opportunity that you
alone can do something about. Certainly you will want to keep
after the field sales manager and headquarters to give you the
things you need—but don't depend on it for opportunity. If
you do, you will never really realize your goals and objectives.

E. The last item of knowledge as a prerequisite to good
   personal organization is an understanding of your specific job assignment. Most any salesman will tell you
   that his job assignment is getting orders, one way or
   another. But oddly enough, you wouldn't believe it if
   you followed many of them about and watched how
   they conducted their activities. That doesn't mean to
   say that these men are doing a bad job. It's just that
   they could do much better if they really understood
   their assignments. Here are some examples of misread-
   ing job assignments:

   1. Some salesmen spend an inordinate amount of time
      trying to find out what their competition is doing.
      But their assignment does not call for, nor are they
      being paid for, espionage.
   2. Other salesmen expend much effort in trying to find
      inequities in their program, their merchandising and
      selling tools, instead of trying to improve their own
      use of them. Very few selling assignments specify
      critical appraisal of products and programs.
   3. Some salesmen are "pickers and choosers" in that
      they decide what they will be good at selling and
      what not. They often ignore opportunity. Assign-
      ments usually specify "across the board" selling.

In understanding a specific job assignment, one must not
only know what he is expected to do and to accomplish, but

also how he is expected to do it. Notice we say "expected." Analysis of a job doesn't mean how the job is being done, but how it is expected to be done—and that's different. It is possible to improvise on a job assignment, as in music, but only if you know the original melody.

The first step toward analyzing a specific selling assignment is the job writeup. Here is an example:

Wholesale Salesman

Under the direction of the National Wholesale Sales Manager, conducts and coordinates all activities necessary to the promotion and sale of specified company products to and through designated wholesale accounts.

1. Establishes and maintains a specified schedule for making wholesaler contacts for the purpose of making direct wholesale sales; such schedule must provide sufficient flexibility to allow for any special wholesale service calls required.

2. Establishes and maintains a specified schedule for making indirect retailer contacts for the purposes of making turnover sales, servicing retail outlets, and policing company wholesale distribution.

3. Prepares and submits to Sales Division headquarters all orders placed with him by the wholesalers and copies of turnover orders from retailers. Follows up on all orders and endeavors, within policy limitations, to assure complete customer satisfaction.

4. Is alert to and informs the Wholesale Sales Manager of special promotional and merchandising opportunities which arise as a result of meetings, programs and conventions of wholesalers in his territory.

5. Cooperates as requested in the planning, development and execution of specialized wholesale promotional programs to augment, complement and otherwise promote the sale of company products through the wholesale distributors.

6. Performs such specific and personal promotional activities as are needed to adequately support the wholesaler in his efforts to sell company products. Such activities include:

    a. The conduct of regular training sessions for the wholesale salesmen, including the making of instructional calls with the salesman when practicable.

    b. Assist wholesaler in maintenance of proper inventory records to whatever degree is practicable and possible. Make appropriate recommendations regarding inventory levels, order size, minimum stock quantities, reorder point, etc., as records and inventory flow indicate.

    c. Maintain knowledge and assist wholesaler in use and distribution of displays and other promotional items.

    d. Conduct of other desirable promotional activities, such as entertainment, within appropriate limits, of wholesale salesmen, buyers and other persons influential in the promotion of sales of company products.

7. Maintains and submits such records, reports and expense accounts as are required by the Sales Division Headquarters and as requested by the National Wholesale Sales Manager.

8. Is alert to matters and reports on appropriate occasion, or as requested, concerning new wholesale business opportunities, pertinent competitive activity, reactions and attitudes of wholesale dealers and others toward the company, its products, policies and its merchandising programs.

This is a typical but simple job writeup and can be used as a model for your own job writeup. Let's examine it briefly.

Note that the lead-off mentions *promotion* and then *sales*—"coordinates all activities necessary to the *promotion* and *sale*. . . ." This would imply that the salesman must "do" much of the promoting and that the sale which the salesman makes to the wholesaler follows the promotional activity with the wholesaler. The lead-off also indicates that two kinds of selling are required by specifying "to and through."

The salesman has to "service" the wholesaler account by holding wholesale sales meetings, helping with inventory control, working with wholesale salesmen, taking turnover orders for the wholesaler while working alone, and in many other ways.

Depending, of course, on how the salesman's compensation program is structured, actually the only thing that pays off for the salesman is the wholesale order itself. Therefore, the salesman in this case has to determine for himself how much "service" time he can invest with each of his wholesale accounts.

"Promotion" in the sense it is used here doesn't mean company advertising, retailer deals, or consumer offers. These things are program tools. The "promotion" refers to *what the salesman does and says* in the nature of pointing up opportunity for the wholesaler—ideas and plans he suggests to the wholesaler for the resale of his merchandise. Certainly the salesman must understand his wholesaler's salesmen—their duties and their capacities.

It is quite obvious that in this job writeup assignment the salesman would not be getting many orders if he spent his time jumping from wholesaler to wholesaler with his order book open. The writeup suggests that unless the salesman promotes with the wholesaler and services his account he will not realize his potential. Some selling, however, does require high-spotting —so-called missionary selling. The introduction of a new product, backed by heavy advertising, might require a "fast-sell" technique. But in this instance—no. In most instances—no. The salesman here has a serious organizing and planning job to do and it demands ingenuity to do it wisely and well.

If you have a job writeup, study it. It can provide a good guide for organizing your time and effort. If you don't have a job writeup, make one for yourself. Make it as detailed as you can, describing everything you do. Study it and inventory the amount of time you estimate that you spend on each element. You might just find yourself busy on unprofitable things.

Star the things that can improve your performance. Plan your time schedules and concentrate your thinking in ways to better do the things that will contribute more to today's bank balance and tomorrow's ambitions.

We will proceed from this point in developing the records that will aid immeasurably in organizing your time and efforts.

Now, however, without going further in examining our example of a job writeup, let's prepare one for you. If your company has already provided you with an assignment outline you can skip this and proceed to the analysis section of this study. If not, using the example as a guide, make your own job writeup:

1. Specify who you report to and write a general statement of your overall duties.
2. Outline your major duty or responsibility. It represents the principal source of your income.
3. Outline corollary assignments that directly contribute to accomplishment of your major responsibility.
4. Outline additional duties that indirectly contribute to accomplishment of your major assignment.

It will take time to prepare your own job writeup but when you finish after giving it plenty of thought, you will have described your job as you see it. You are now ready to analyze your own job with the objective of becoming better organized to better accomplish its goals. Answer these questions:

1. What is the major assignment?
2. Can this assignment be accomplished by a direct one-time or repeat selling effort on your part only?
3. Does the assignment require services on your part, such as inventorying, detailing, etc., to realize final results?
4. Does the assignment require your enlistment of the aid of others, such as clerks, delivery or warehouse men, service men, salesmen?
5. Are you required to do many things you do not feel you are being paid for that do not seem to relate to improving your job?

After you have given thought to these questions and answered them satisfactorily for yourself, you are ready to make time assessments. Count the number of various things that you do, i.e., selling, interviews, traveling, reporting, clerk and salesmen training, detailing, inventorying, etc. Take a forty-four hour week and give a time assignment to each element in the following manner:

1. Give half the time to the major responsibility and two or three contributing responsibilities.
2. Divide the other half of your time to other duties in order of their importance.

This effort has equipped you to plan your time in a better way to realize your opportunities by giving you a better idea of what these opportunities are.

In this chapter we have used our knowledge and experience to give us a head start in personal organization for a greater contribution to today's bank balance and tomorrow's ambitions. We shall now translate this organization to meaningful records and the use of these records for more effective personal planning.

6

How to Develop and Use
A Dynamic Record System Geared
To Your Own Selling Requirements

Consistently usable records are worth their weight in gold to the ingenious salesman. Unintelligible, impractical, unnecessary records are a severe handicap. There isn't one salesman in ten who has records that will permit realizing full potential.

Record keeping is the bane of most salesmen's existence. It's a chore and a bore. The average salesman finishes his last call of the day at 5:30 P.M. and it takes him a half hour or an hour to get to his motel or home. He is hungry and tired and faces at least an hour of record keeping, writing orders and reports, correspondence and organization for the next day.

If he is away from home the temptation of a cocktail and dinner and a movie, to get away from it all, is very great. It is easy to put off record keeping until morning—when it never gets done.

If he is at home his wife has a few duties scheduled—repairing something or reprimanding the children. She wants him to relax and be in good humor and usually won't let him get right at his record keeping chores.

Record keeping and daily call organization is, without doubt, an absolute necessity for the salesman and the problem of getting at it and completing it well, is a matter of personal dependability. He must promise himself that he will do it, organize himself to do it, and stick with it—and no exceptions.

A good daily routine: A light to medium breakfast at 8 A.M. A nourishing luncheon (alone) at noon. A light snack, with something sweet, like hot chocolate, at 3 P.M. Dinner at 7:30. The average salesman cannot afford the time luxury of luncheon or dinner entertaining. It should be indulged in only on an occasion. Even twenty-minute coffee breaks are an intrusion on time and money. Camaraderie with customers and clerks must be treated very carefully as it can often be more hurtful than helpful. The line between being pleasant and likable and being intimate is a thin one to be avoided. Your family understands you; your customers do not.

Under this routine, record keeping takes an hour, 6:30–7:30 P.M., each evening including Friday, and 8:00–9:00 A.M. Saturday. Mail orders and reports to headquarters on Tuesdays, Thursdays and Saturdays. Golf, boating, fishing and other relaxation can be indulged in on weekends, but keep an hour or so for business reading on Sunday evenings. During the week keep up with the news—your business conversation must be timely.

Now back to the records. First come the company records. These are based upon what the company wants to know about how you are operating. Unfortunately, except for reference, these records generally are not of much value to you. Let's face it—your company wants to know:

1. If you are putting in a full day of work every day as shown by your daily report showing number of calls that day and a record of accomplishments.
2. Your effectiveness; i.e., your ratio of orders to calls, and number of orders to order size. This information can be obtained from the daily report.
3. Your adherence to the program, which can be ascertained by the number of current deals or offers you report on your daily report.
4. Where you are planning to go for business as covered by your routing report.

5. How well you are covering your territory, as indicated by a comparison of your daily report with your routing schedule.
6. How efficient you are with the company's money, as your expense report will show.
7. How well organized you are, as covered by special test reports.

Unfortunately, these reports do not benefit you very much. Nor, except in a limited way, do they aid you in planning your time and learning where to apply your efforts. The records you need must provide you quickly with the following information:

1. Account Information
   a. Names of people who are important in your business relations and, if possible, a few of their individual likes and dislikes, plus a comment or two about their personalities. These would include clerks, buyers, merchandise managers, advertising and display managers, and management people.
   b. Credit and collection information.
   c. Merchandising information—dates and character of special sales events—promotions—advertising and display policies—areas of cooperation with you and with your competitor.
   d. Past purchase record.
   e. Current and running invoice purchase record.
   f. Your products' sales performances.

2. Territory Information
   a. Account listings by area within the territory; both the accounts you sell *and* the accounts that carry your type of products but not yours. These are retail accounts and both direct and indirect (through the wholesaler) should be listed.
   b. Routing planning work form. This shows where you have been, how much was accomplished and what remains to be accomplished in the new term.

    c. Physical routing information such as parking information with the number of accounts that can be covered from one parking location. Highway, street, and location information. Store hours and afternoons closed.

3. Business Increase Information
    a. Preferred prospect listing with reasons why preferred.
    b. Economic factors (both good and bad) in areas within your territory that could affect your business in those areas.

These are records that will be used on a day-to-day, call-by-call basis. They are personal records, but few companies prepare their salesmen with a complete and daily usable record form. Therefore, these records must be a project of the salesman's own volition. They must be kept up on a daily basis—at the same time company daily reports are recorded.

We are going to outline and illustrate a record form that is valuable on a call-to-call basis and will form the background for organization of the territory coverage and work plan. Here is an outline of the record:

1. The form is a loose-leaf notebook incorporating 8½ x 11 heavy stock paper printed forms. This book will be your personal record, kept up to date and carried with you at all times.

2. Each sheet, front and back, is one dealer record form kept by area within the territory. The number of dealers involved dictates the number of separate and individual loose-leaf books. With relatively few dealers, there might be only one book for the whole territory. With many dealers there might be a book for each area within the territory. In a city an area might be bounded by streets. In country territories, it might be by geography within counties.

3. If several loose-leaf books are involved they can be organized so that only two books are required during any one weekly trip. Areas should be quite small with perhaps 35 to 40 deal-

ers. With such a small number of dealers the sheets can be organized by routing patterns rather than alphabetically.

4. Here's an organization example of the record: A territory consists of 160 active direct retailers of whom 30 are major accounts. In addition, there are five wholesalers, all of whom are major accounts, and 1,800 accounts (including members of chains) that carry a little of the line, *either* yours or your competitor's or both, and who buy through the wholesaler. Of these 1,800 accounts, 400 of them do 80 per cent of the whole-sale indirect business.

   a. The record for this territory would provide a sheet for each of the 160 direct accounts, each of the 400 major indirect accounts, and each of the 5 wholesalers. These 565 accounts would be segregated into 14 areas with approximately 40 accounts per area. The 1,400 smaller indirect accounts would *not* appear. Remember now that many of these 400 major indirect (wholesale) accounts may not even be carrying your line. Some of them may be direct accounts of your competitors. Nevertheless, each account in this category does a good business in your type of line.

   b. Loose-leaf Book #1 would incorporate separate sheets for the 30 major retail accounts and the 5 wholesale accounts plus 5 or 10 near-major accounts. This book would be used for territory high-spotting purposes at the introduction of a new program. (Note, two identical record sheets should be provided for each of these major accounts— one for the major account book and another for the area book.)

   c. Books #2 through #6 would each include three adjacent routing areas with 40 or so account sheets for each area.

   d. A tabbed index sheet for each of the three areas in each of the books would be an information sheet on the area itself with notes concerning business prospects, routing, parking, etc. This area index sheet can be used as a routing/planning work sheet. (Figure 6-1)

   e. Account sheets for new accounts or additions to each area and the territory can be added as conditions warrant. Obviously, sheets should also be taken out as conditions warrant.

5. Here's a listing of information on each dealer sheet (Figure 6-2):

   a. Name, billing address, telephone number of account. (Telephone numbers only on direct accounts.)

   b. Name, shipping address, telephone number of account. (Only if different from billing address.)

   c. For chain stores there would be a master sheet showing buying headquarters, warehouse locations, store locations and listings. Only if a branch store required a *selling* and servicing call, not merely a *policing only* call, would a *separate* sheet be included in the proper area book for the branch.

   d. Past five years' purchase record (this section would be marked *"indirect"* for those accounts with no record).

   e. Current year *invoice* record (space provided for a five-year period). On direct accounts, factory invoices would be posted weekly. On indirect accounts, turnover orders *taken by you* would be posted.

   f. "Buys through" space for the name of the wholesaler who services indirect accounts. This space also for those direct accounts that do some buying through the wholesaler. ·

   g. Space for names of people and people information.

   h. Credit and collection record and information. Space for recording current information.

   i. Space for merchandising and promotional information to be posted currently.

   j. Type or classification of account (drug, stationery, department store).

Figure 6-2 is a form example which should be projected to 8½ x 11 size and punched for loose-leaf book use. As you study the form, go back to the written explanation of each section in the form for clearer understanding. This record is presented as a pattern only. It will fill the needs of many salesmen but many others will have to alter it to suit their individual requirements. Only after you have studied the form carefully and have understood it completely should you move on to the explanation of how you put the record together.

ACCOUNT LISTING AREA INDEX

Area #_____

Approx. No.
of Accts._____   Terr. #_____

Description of Area: Bounded on the North, etc. -- Comprises, etc. --_____

_____

_____

Routing Information: _____

_____

_____

_____

_____

_____

Business Information: _____

_____

_____

_____

_____

_____

Area Routing Date Record: _____thru_____. _____thru_____.

_____thru_____. _____thru_____. _____thru_____.

_____thru_____. _____thru_____. _____thru_____.

Figure 6-1. (front)

ACCOUNT LISTING AREA INDEX

Accounts Listed in this Area #_____

Name   Address

_____   _____
_____   _____
_____   _____
_____   _____
_____   _____
_____   _____
_____   _____
_____   _____
_____   _____
_____   _____
_____   _____
_____   _____
_____   _____
_____   _____
_____   _____
_____   _____
_____   _____
_____   _____
_____   _____
_____   _____
_____   _____

Figure 6-1. (back)

ACCOUNT LISTING RECORD   Terr. #_____

Area # _____

☐ Wholesale   ☐ Direct   ☐ Indirect

Type _____

Name _____   Name _____

Billing Address _____   Shipping Address _____

Telephone _____   Telephone _____

Current Purchase Record   Past Purchases

Year	Date	Inv. #	Amount	Date	Inv. #	Amount		

Buys through:

Call Dates: Check for Routing

Year ___ ___ ___

Year ___ ___ ___

(for chain store master record use – back for branch store listings)

Figure 6-2. (front)

ACCOUNT LISTING RECORD

PEOPLE INFORMATION:

	Name	Position	For Information
1.			
2.			
3.			
4.			
5.			

Credit and Collection Information: _____

Merchandising and Promotion Information: _____

Branch Store Listings:

Figure 6-2. (back)

Rereading the material preceding the account forms, area forms, and routing forms is again suggested if there is a question at all on makeup. We will now discuss: a) How we get the information for completing the dealer listing and area forms, b) How we use the information for instant and effective routing, c) How we use the information for ingenious call-by-call selling. It's all a part of good personal organization.

a) *Getting the information*

You must make up the form that is best for you. It should contain the information that you need at your fingertips on every call. A soft-cover, loose-leaf book should be used, with a label on the front for the area numbers.

Take time to construct the form just the way you want it, and then take it to a printer. Consult with him concerning the kind of stock needed and the format. Don't forget that you will want to fill in information by hand on a daily basis while the sheets are *in the book*. Construct your form so that this is easy to do. Order enough forms to last, anticipating adding and exchanging forms. Plan carefully so that you will not have to redo the book.

Start your organizing with the retail and wholesale accounts that you contact direct. Enlist the help of your company in getting the account name and address, purchase record, invoices this year to date, dealer record information on credit and any other information they can give.

Your company should have the names and addresses of all trade classification accounts in your territory that carry and sell your kind of merchandise lines and that you *do not* sell direct. If not, there are other sources. Your wholesalers might let you have their account lists—generally they are not secret, especially if you do detail (turnover) work for them. If you get the wholesale lists, have the wholesale sales manager star the important accounts for both your line and your competitor's line for your listing. You will not record all of the wholesaler's list—just the important accounts.

Three other sources are:

(1) Retailer trade classification mailing listings which you can buy for your areas only. Your company or the local newspaper can give you the names of people who deal in mailing lists.

(2) The local newspaper itself can give you listings (in fact, routings) of drug accounts, stationery accounts, cleaning and dyeing concerns, laundries, supermarkets, etc. However, you will have to consult several newspapers throughout your territory.

(3) Another source is the telephone classified advertising pages —find out from the local telephone company what phone books are printed in your territory and obtain a copy of each as you go around.

Regardless of how you get your listings there will be a lot of culling out to do. In fact, it may take a year to get your area listings just the way you want them. Account listings will require considerable personal investigations—but this personal attention will prove to be a very profitable venture in new business.

After you have your record forms, both index and master listing, printed the way you want them, start completing the forms and organizing them *right away*. Don't worry if the record is not anywhere near the completed record you want. You will complete it as time goes on; meanwhile, you need this kind of personal selling record *now*. You cannot be properly organized without it.

b) *Using your record for instant and effective routing*

Each loose-leaf account record book should be put together by routing area in the following order: (1) Area information and index sheet, (2) Wholesalers, (3) Direct retail accounts that must be called upon each time you visit the area, (4) Direct retail accounts called on less frequently, (5) Indirect retail accounts in some order of their importance.

Do not organize your record alphabetically. You will go through each area section so often that you will know where

TWO-WEEK ROUTING SCHEDULE

1st Week Beginning: _____

	Hotel/Motel	City/State
Salesman_____	_____	_____
Terr. #_____Region_____	_____	_____

	Date	Area #	Accounts from Master Account Listings	
Mon.	_____	_____	_____	_____
	_____	_____	_____	_____
	_____	_____	_____	_____
Tues.	_____	_____	_____	_____
	_____	_____	_____	_____
	_____	_____	_____	_____
Wed.	_____	_____	_____	_____
	_____	_____	_____	_____
	_____	_____	_____	_____
Thurs.	_____	_____	_____	_____
	_____	_____	_____	_____
	_____	_____	_____	_____
Fri.	_____	_____	_____	_____
	_____	_____	_____	_____
	_____	_____	_____	_____

Figure 6-3. (front)

TWO-WEEK ROUTING SCHEDULE

2nd Week Beginning: _____

		Hotel/Motel	City/State
Salesman _____		_____	_____
Terr. #_____ Region_____		_____	_____

	Date	Area #	Accounts from Master Account Listings	
Mon.	_____	_____	_____	_____
	_____	_____	_____	_____
	_____	_____	_____	_____
Tues.	_____	_____	_____	_____
	_____	_____	_____	_____
	_____	_____	_____	_____
Wed.	_____	_____	_____	_____
	_____	_____	_____	_____
	_____	_____	_____	_____
Thurs.	_____	_____	_____	_____
	_____	_____	_____	_____
	_____	_____	_____	_____
Fri.	_____	_____	_____	_____
	_____	_____	_____	_____
	_____	_____	_____	_____

Figure 6-3. (back)

specific account records are located if you have to refer to them. Each record book is a work tool that you will use constantly as you work each area. Order of importance is much more practical in routing and organizing within each area. When you want to find an account all you have to know is the address.

If, following sales meetings and new program announcements, you engage in high-spotting your territory, it is wise to make up a special account book with a duplicate record of the area book listing for that purpose. This, of course, would not be necessary unless you have a long territory listing requiring more than one or two loose-leaf books.

At the end of each day as you make out your daily call report, post the *call date* in the proper space on your account listing record as, for example, 5/16. Place an asterisk * beside the date if you took an order—5/16 *. The order should be indicated whether it is direct or indirect. At the same time, make any changes or record any new information on the record cards as required. Some of this detail can be accomplished while waiting on calls as you work the area. You will carry the proper area record with you always as a part of your "carry in" equipment.

At the end of each week, post your factory invoices. Then, using the suggested routing form (See Figure 6-3) make out your routing for the next week (or two weeks, corrected each week). Simply decide what areas you are going to work in and turn to the appropriate account listing book. Go through the account listings and *pencil* check √ in the call date section each account you intend to visit on this trip. (As you post your calls daily in ink you either erase the pencil √ marks or write the call date right over them.) If you miss a call, the pencilled √ mark remains right there as a reminder the next time you are scheduled for this area.

You know the number of calls you can normally make per day, so by simply counting the pencil √ marks you know the time required in the area. Only check those accounts where you can write business. Where and when you find it convenient, you can perform a policing duty (i.e., checking to see if display is up, etc.) by simply walking in and out of the account—but don't count this as a call. Incidentally, we will later discuss "policing action" as an ingenious selling device to get strong wholesale support.

Don't set a "comfortable" routing schedule. Push yourself a little—an extra call on a prospect, for example. And be certain to give yourself alternate calls for emergencies. Of course, working from a well-organized area book gives you alternate calls at a glance. It helps greatly, too, on those short period call-backs —"I can't see you right now, but could you come back at 10:30?"

Don't base your routing schedule on your "average calls per day" quota. Think of: (1) Where will you go? (2) What do I have to do? (3) How much time will it take? Think of orders and total dollar sales anticipated first. Think of time for each call and time between calls. You will line up to your average calls per day automatically. Now, let's take routing procedure step by step.

1. Decide the area that you are going to work and turn to the appropriate area account listing.
2. Go over each dealer sheet and *pencil* in a check √ mark where there is business to be taken.
3. Count the marks (suppose out of 40 accounts, you checked 19) and roughly determine the number of days' work involved. (If your actual call average is seven per day, you would have three days' work with a little opportunity for new account free-lancing.)
4. Now take a routing form and go back to the beginning and allocate the calls to days (i.e., Monday, Tuesday, etc.) by estimating the time required for each call including travel.
5. Select another area and repeat the procedure to fill out the week.

It is suggested that a two-week routing be made each week as illustrated in the form. In this way follow-ups and adjustments can be made to keep the routing more accurate. Effective routing, i.e., being in the right account at the right time, is an essential element of ingenious selling.

c) *Using your account record as a call-by-call selling aid*

Just prior to and during a selling call, it is wise to refer to your account listing record for the following information and its use:

1. Names and positions of people. In your selling interview you will want to refer to people, from warehouse man and clerk to merchandise manager, *by name.*
2. Date you took last order. Was it confirmed? Was it altered by the store?
3. Invoice date and amount. How much has been sold? Turnover rate?
4. Credit and collection information. Are there invoices outstanding that would prevent order taking? Do you need credit references?
5. Promotional and display and advertising information. Does the account normally have a special event that your current program would fit?
6. Past years' purchase record. Is the account keeping up to former years? Gaining or losing ground?

From all of this information and with careful thought you set an objective for each particular call. You determine how you are going to conduct the interview. For example: Your *objective* may be to increase this account's purchases from you 10 per cent on a yearly basis. To do this, you may have to take three more orders this year and each will have to be $350.00 or more to increase 10 per cent the orders taken last year.

To *accomplish* this, you will have to get two extra feet of counter display from your competitors and the lion's share of the store advertising and promotional support in display and clerk effort.

You determine that the best *procedure* will be to go after the advertising and promotional effort first, on the basis that the lion's potential for the store justifies that effort. The increased orders will follow to support the increased promotional activity.

Without good records you cannot be properly organized to take advantage of the extra potential waiting for you. It is a rare company that has a personal record system for its salesmen that is of real field value. Company reports and records are largely of value from the company standpoint only.

A requirement of ingenious selling is the development of a valuable personal record system and using the record as a tool to exploit each territory area for the extra true potential that it holds.

We shall now return to our inventory taking—this time to the natural skills necessary for realizing true earnings possibilities.

7

Taking Inventory of Your
Natural Skills for Ingenious Selling...
Conversational Ability,
Persuasion and Perception

In this chapter and the next, we will inventory and exploit your natural selling skills. We previously identified your natural selling talents as confidence, attitude and organization. These are tools of the trade. We now identify conversation, persuasion and perception as the natural skills in using those tools for more successful selling.

Our first consideration will be to determine how well your natural selling skills have already been developed. This we will accomplish with a three-part inventory.

Item No. 1—How skilled a conversationalist are you? Can you direct conversation both in a group and with only one other person? Although we will delve into social as well as business conversation, keep in mind that we regard the selling interview as *directed conversation.*

Item No. 2—How skilled at persuasion are you? Have you been able to swing people around to your point of view both in social and business situations? In selling, how much do the things you *do* influence the sale as compared to the things you *have,* such as adver-

tising, products, program? If you are depending on
the things you have almost exclusively, you are not
even beginning to achieve your potential.

Item No. 3—How skilled at perception are you? How well do
you catch the clues that direct the selling interview to a successful conclusion? How well do you
stay on the right track by correctly perceiving the
buyer's reaction? Perception in a selling sense is
a natural attribute, but yet it is one that can be
developed as a powerful skill in bringing each sale
to a rewarding end.

Back to Item No. 1. We shall first take inventory of your:

Conversational Skills

We have already defined the selling interview as "directed
conversation." Before we dissect the selling interview, then,
we might determine just how good at conversation you are.
You have to know what foundation you have to work with
before you can start to build.

There are courses of study in conversation. For social conversation, The Ethel Cotton Course in Conversation is an example. For business conversation, Jesse S. Nirenberg's Workshop in Persuasive Communication is one that comes to mind.
Handling specific social and business situations via word-power
is a subject that has been explored by writers and lecturers.
Pursuit of your improvement in conversational ability is most
certainly recommended.

But in the light of using word power in a selling sense,
both the writer and lecturer have had an opportunity to prepare. In addition, they have a captive audience who mostly
either can't or won't talk back. You can dispute the words and
ideas in these pages to little avail so far as the author is concerned. If you write your objections, the author has ample time
to prepare a rebuttal. A salesman, in a selling situation, has no
such opportunity.

The doctor can take time with most diagnoses—the patient doesn't go away. He may often take hours or even days to consult with other physicians. The attorney may spend much time preparing his "briefs." He may get an extension of time to get his case in order. Even in court, he may ask for a recess to reassemble his arguments.

But the salesman must have the answer right now—no waiting—and it must be phrased properly and explained clearly or he loses the order. The salesman usually has but a few minutes in front of a buyer who surrounds himself with untold elements of distraction—telephones, clerks, customers, to name a tiny few—plus, we are sorry to relate, a tendency to be distracted. No wonder sales in the best interests of the buyer are lost and other sales are but poorly and incompletely made!

Sparkling conversation holds interest and attention like nothing else can. A skilled sales conversationalist practicing the art of directed conversation can provide a stimulating and profitable few minutes for any buyer. Now, however, the purpose of this specific discussion is to determine just how conversationally adept you are—by taking inventory. At the same time, we will want to give the whole subject some objective thought, coming back in the next chapter to exploit our conversational skills. Let's probe a little and start making a few notes.

1. Have you in high school, college, or on your own taken courses or engaged in extra-curricular activity in speech, theater, debating, forensics, conversation, public speaking? If you have, you have learned some basic principles that make it simpler to engage in effective "directed" sales conversation.

Write down on your note pad the formal courses you can relate to conversation from among those mentioned and any others. Include sales training courses or such things as a Dale Carnegie course. Now include participation in activities such as the Toastmasters Club or political organizations where you are required to get on your feet for comment.

Go back over your notes with this question—have any of these things helped me with my need for expressing myself better?

Keep in mind that in selling you must use conversation to explain and persuade toward a definite goal. Being able to express yourself well in all matters aids your selling purpose.

Now make a note for reference later to give additional thought for your need of more formal effective conversation builders. This book recommends "learn as you earn" methods and there will be additional tips on strengthening your conversational ability as we progress. Nevertheless, after you take inventory and exploit more sophisticated ingenious selling techniques, you may decide upon reviewing basic material. Right now let's get back to the inventory.

2. In social conversation—

    a. Do you talk a lot or little?
    b. Monopolize the conversation?
    c. Are you a good listener?
    d. Does your mind wander?
    e. Do you almost always catch what others are saying?
    f. Do you remember names and dates?
    g. Do others seek out your opinion?
    h. Do you have the feeling that others are listening when you talk?

Write down the answers to these questions about your social conversation. Answer honestly and think through each question thoroughly. Here's how you can find out much about your adeptness as a conversationalist:

a. If you join in the conversation and have an opinion about a lot of things, this is good. In selling you have to "carry" the conversation and being a good talker is an asset. If you score yourself as talking too little make a reminder note to practice forcing yourself into more social conversation.

b. Monopolizing the conversation isn't just talking a lot. It insults your companions by insinuating that they don't have any opinions or ideas of their own. If you do this in social conversation, chances are you are overbearing in sales conversation. Make a reminder note.

c. You can't be a good talker unless you are a good listener too. You must concentrate on what the other speaker is saying so that you will know when to interject and what to interject with. Make a note.

d. People's minds wander because they fight boredom and try to occupy themselves with their own thoughts. If this is a cause of bad listening or talking (people often talk without knowing what they are saying), you will have to do some work on it. Make a note.

e. Here we distinguish between listening, your mind wandering, and simply following points in order. The speaker makes a point, you speculate on it (as opposed to your mind wandering on another subject) and before you have it absorbed, the speaker has made another point you have missed. In sales conversation this is usually not a problem because points are made by speakers one at a time. However, mind training in this regard is helpful. Make a note.

f. Remembering names and dates is important to sales conversation. It permits a smooth flow of presentation and enables you to highlight previous promotional successes and people responsible within both your and the buyer's organization. Testimonial type selling is very effective. A good memory in all matters requires constant review and work. Make a note.

g. If your social friends seek your opinion you have an asset worth developing in selling. That asset is respect in your field. The knowledge and experience you gain can be translated immediately into results because you already have a knack of getting people to seek you out and accept your advice. This is something to work for and you should make a note accordingly.

h. Are you interesting? Do you express yourself well? The answers lie with others. Your only clue is your reaction as to whether your listeners "get it." If you get a feeling that in social conversation no one pays much attention to what you say, you will have to engage in some long practice sessions for your selling conversation. This will appear in later chapters. Make a note.

Don't confuse all of these things with sociability. You don't have to be a social lion or a hail fellow well met as a prerequisite for sales success. In fact, being a bit anti-social might even be helpful. Sociability is not being questioned nor are we concerned with it—only social conversation.

3. In conversations with your fellow salesmen or in other business conversations—

   a. Do you get into the thick of it?
   b. Do you have something to say on almost every subject—and do you say it?
   c. Do you let others have their say before you jump in?
   d. Do you feel others listen to your opinions?
   e. Do you most often get agreement? (Next subject is persuasion.)
   f. Do you feel others understand quickly what you are trying to explain?

Here again, make notes as you did in social conversation. Your fellow salesmen are "sounding boards" for building many sales techniques and especially so in the "bull session" type of get-together. How you answer each question as you recall the situation will give you a lead as to your present ability as a sales conversationalist:

   a. This shows your eagerness and interest.
   b. This reflects your knowledge and experience.
   c. This shows your adroitness in directed conversation.
   d. This establishes the degree of respect you have earned.
   e. This shows your aptness at persuasion.
   f. This measures your degree of expressiveness.

Business conversation is not necessarily sales directed conversation, but it is a good clue to judging one's talent as an attention-getter and holder and a forceful conversationalist. Think about the above questions one by one to reach some conclusions about your business conversation ability.

Now that we have explored both social and business conversation, we shall attempt a rating for general conversation. How do you rate yourself: Excellent, Good, or Fair?

1. My choice of words and vocabulary.	E	G	F
2. I get attention during conversation.	E	G	F
3. I listen carefully while others are talking.	E	G	F
4. My conversational explanations seem to be clear to others.	E	G	F
5. Others ask my opinion.	Often	Occasionally	Seldom
6. Ideas come to me during conversation.	Often	Occasionally	Seldom
7. I often reserve my opinion.	Yes	No	
8. With questions and remarks I feel that I "lead" conversation.	Yes	No	
9. After conversation, I often think of things I should have said.	Yes	No	

If you have been thinking over all of these questions on social, business and general conversation and trying to give yourself honest answers, you now have at least a fair idea of how you personally rank as a conversationalist. Don't hold "tongue in cheek" if you've ranked yourself pretty high—most salesmen are interesting people and their conversational knack is well known. Unfortunately, many do not translate their good conversational ability to their sales effort. Result, their sales effort seems drab and lackluster.

If you rank yourself as only fair as a conversationalist, you should try:

1. Self-study or a "Making friends, influencing people" course to improve.
2. Keeping abreast of current news events and discussing them in depth with family members and friends is a "hurry up" conversational ability builder.
3. Adding new words to your vocabulary on a day-to-day basis through reading is really important for anyone engaged in selling.

A lot of "you" goes into the sales interview. Much of the difference between superior and average sales performances is a projection of individual personality factors into the sales effort. A sales situation is a discussional or conversational situation. In the next chapter we shall pursue the further development of this natural skill.

With this objective inventory of your conversational ability, you will be better equipped to apply your talents to the "directed conversational" skills required in successful selling.

The Persuasion Factor

Let's move on to an inventory of one more of the natural skills —persuasiveness. Certainly, if we intend to sell anything we must be persuasive; and to the extent we are persuasive, to that extent are we convincing. The dictionary definition is interesting.

Persuade—To win over by entreaty or reasoning, or by appeal. To endeavor to influence.

Synonyms—Allure, coax, convince, dispose, entice, impel, incite, incline, induce, influence, lead, move, urge, win.

Of these words, convince alone has no direct reference to moving the will, denoting an effect upon the understanding only; we may be convinced of truth that has no manifest connection with duty or action.

> To persuade is to bring the will of another to a desired decision by some influence upon it short of compulsion.

Some people are naturally more persuasive than others—why? They learned how, probably better and earlier. Persuasion is a learned skill—mostly by natural means. A child may have been brought up in an environment which required that he be persuasive or he would not get the things he wanted. A young person after high school or college is thrown into a work situation that requires good "people" relations and a necessity for "selling" ideas. Marriage requires persuasive qualities on both sides.

So, before we take inventory, let it be said that anyone's persuasive qualities can be improved immeasurably and there are definite ways to do it. We shall go into that in a later chapter. Let's first see how well our persuasive talents are developed.

In your everyday affairs, you know without realizing it how persuasive you are. You can tell by the persuasive problems you accept and those you avoid or reject. For example, you might be willing to visit a small loan company for a high interest loan but avoid a bank to ask for an unsecured note. Yet you may know that if your credit is good you stand a chance of getting the money at a fraction of the cost. How many traffic fines are paid by people who feel they have a case for court but who doubt if they could convince the judge?

However, in measuring this skill, and partly because it is a learned one, let's go right to the sales interview.

1. How well are you able to get the buyer's attention and hold it? In some way you must persuade the buyer to listen. Pick out any three calls you made today and recall your opening remarks and each buyer's response. *Write them down.* Did you get the buyer with you? Now, thinking about it, did the buyer seem to stay with you? *At this point he might have been totally unsold, but that doesn't make any difference if you persuaded him to participate in the interview.*

2. How well are you able to get the buyer to accept the facts about your proposition? You must persuade the buyer to weigh

or consider your offer. On the calls you selected see if you can recall one or two of your most telling arguments for your proposition and the buyer's response. Did the buyer seem to be giving your offer consideration or did he act disinterested? *At this point the buyer may still be unsold—but what matters is that you have persuaded him to consider.*

3. How well are you able to get the buyer to give you a favorable response? You must now persuade the buyer to consider your offer in a favorable manner. On the calls you have drawn upon try and recall the first inkling of either a favorable or a negative response. Of course, a negative response doesn't mean a lost sale, because with some buyers a negative response is only a defense mechanism. After this first response, did the buyer seem to be still considering your proposition? *You now know how well you have persuaded the buyer to let you attempt other tactics and selling techniques.*

4. How well are you able to get the buyer to give you a favorable decision? *You must finally persuade the buyer not to say "no."* He, of course, doesn't have to say "yes" to give you the favorable decision that he is ready to buy. We will want to discuss the "double positive" close and the "negative decision being positive" close. For the moment now, however, recall your selected interviews and determine how well you persuaded your buyers to bring your sales to a positive conclusion.

Remember now, don't say to yourself, "I've had pretty good success in getting orders. I must have good persuasive ability. How else would I get them?" The answer is that you can get orders in many ways other than convincing the buyer to buy. The most obvious is that he may be giving you orders without your asking—and you may be failing to get him to buy enough.

We shall specifically discuss the development of this skill of persuasion in the following chapter. Before that, you should have knowledge of your present ability. Try this suggestion:

At the end of each working day next week select three calls at random, two successful, one failure, and write them down.

Give yourself a rating on part of each call—E for Excellent, 8 points, F for Fair, 6 points, P for Poorly, 1 point for trying.

Sales Action   *Rating*

1. Getting immediate attention.
2. Getting buyer attention "back on track."
3. Holding buyer attention throughout.
4. Getting sales arguments accepted.
5. Getting buyer interest in offer.
6. Holding buyer interest in offer.
7. Getting buyer interest "back on track."
8. Getting favorable response.
9. Holding buyer interest on a favorable level.
10. Holding interest while employing new arguments.
11. Withholding a negative decision.
12. Obtaining a positive decision.

In the first few of these tests you will be inclined to rate yourself well even if you failed to get an order. Somewhere along the line your powers of persuasion were remiss, so check again. A score of 72 is passing, 96 would be exceptionally persuasive.

However, if you do rate yourself as excellent, you can check on yourself in other ways.

1. You will also be adroit at winning arguments in social situations and still maintain close friendships.
2. Your opinion on a variety of problems will be sought after by business acquaintances and friends.
3. You will be a decision-maker.
4. Your home life will be well-managed.
5. You will be known as a "comer" in your business.

Adeptness in the art of persuasion will already have shown its accomplishments. It becomes a part of personality and cannot be just confined to the selling situation. For this reason, strengthening your skill at persuasion will require practicing techniques in social, business, and selling situations. And no matter how good you become in using this skill, you will never be completely satisfied with the results.

Now, we come to another skill that aids greatly our conversational skills and persuasion skills to pay off. Let us examine the:

Perception Factor

Perception is more than awareness. But it incorporates awareness. It is more a developed sense of direction finding. Like the traffic cop at the five-street intersection. Perception opens the way—clears the path.

To find out how good at perception you are isn't easy, but it is necessary before you can properly develop this essential skill. Development comes in the next chapter. Let's begin your inventory of perceptional skill with examples and illustrations.

Example No. 1. Women are very probably more perceptive than men. Why? Because they have to be. They have to be attuned to the reactions of men because they depend upon the male of the species as the head and provider of the household. Women want to keep their men in the right frame of mind to continue to be productive and agreeable. We can learn much from women about perception.

Have you ever noticed that women will very seldom answer a direct question. They have trained themselves not to do it. If you ask your wife, "Doris, what do we have for dinner?" she will say, "Are you hungry, dear?" She won't tell you that it's roast lamb for fear you'll say, "What again!" She waits to find out if you're hungry and in case you are she'll tell you. If you are not very hungry and so indicate, she will go into a long dissertation about how she found this delicious looking lamb roast at a wonderful bargain and even though you had lamb on Sunday she just couldn't afford to pass it up.

Maybe you're not happy with the lamb roast but you're not going to upset a wife who is looking after your interests by doing careful shopping. She knows this but she doesn't know what tact to take until she can put her perception to work. That's why women don't answer direct questions.

Here are some typical husband questions and wife answers. See if you can perceive the reasons for the wife's answer.

Q. Are you going to the grocery store now?
A. Would you like to go along? Is there something I can get for you?

Q. Are you going to play bridge again this afternoon?
A. Is there something you would like me to do for you today?

Q. Would you like to see that movie at the Strand?
A. I don't know if I can get a sitter tonight.

Q. When is your brother going to get a job and leave?
A. Charlie, you know that cute dress at Fields priced at only $90.00 that I told you about. I've decided *not* to get it after all.

If you can come up with logical reasons for the wife's answers, with an explanation as in Example No. 1, you have developed a sense of perception.

A passing comment: Women have more emotional reactions to everyday situations than do men and women buyers are much more perceptive of salesmen's attitudes than are men buyers. For this reason a directed sales conversation with women buyers is more difficult than with men. They are more perceptive to the salesman's reactions than he is to theirs.

Example No. 2. Buyers have developed a defense mechanism against the salesman's perception of their reactions. They maintain silence and if asked a question often reply with a negative answer. They adopt a "prove it to me" attitude that is difficult to break through to discover how well you are doing. Many invite distractions. Some assume a flippant attitude. And on and on. Actually, these things are not in character with the buyer's true personality but, nevertheless, they make perception by the salesman a problem to be solved.

A salesman of a well-advertised line of lawn and garden supplies has been advised that a neighborhood shop has been getting calls for his brand of weed killer. The shop carries full lines of competitive garden supplies. The salesman reasons that he should not sell only the weed killer, but his complete line. He knows the buyer will resist investment in the whole line, but he also knows that the store needs that weed killer badly.

During the interview the buyer is adamant. He wants the weed killer but he won't add another complete line. However, the salesman seems to get attention when he suggests a test. He implies that his line could eventually replace a slower selling, less profitable line that would make the temporary increase in investment worthwhile. Only a test can prove it—buying the weed killer alone won't determine anything. The buyer already knows that will sell fast.

Questions of perception: How does the salesman know if he is on the right track? How should he proceed with the sale? Are more selling points necessary or is this the time to close? Does the buyer understand the offer?

Write down the method or methods you would use to get a reaction from the buyer that would supply you with the answers to the above questions. Do not read on until you have done this.

In reviewing your method, keep in mind that knowing how to get reactions from your buyers is a part of the skill of perception itself. The other part is knowing how to read the reaction correctly.

Now to grade yourself:

1. Did your method incorporate questions that would indicate the buyer's interest in the offer and the degree of interest? A *yes* answer is 50 points.

2. Did your method include a dramatic approach to the problem, such as the salesman starting to put away his samples and close up his equipment? A *yes* answer is 50 points.

3. Did your method suggest that the salesman briefly review the offer, such as, "Mr. Buyer, although I have mentioned these things once, I would like to put them in focus again. First. . . ." A *yes* answer is 50 points.

4. Did your method employ some means of asking for the order or a decision? A *yes* answer is 50 points.

One hundred points would be using good approaches toward getting buyer reaction. Using No. 1 is the least that can be done, and it is very necessary. Depending on the type of dramatics, No. 2 is usually quite dangerous at this stage. However, if circumstances warrant, it can be used. Employing No. 3 is just good selling. The strong points must be re-emphasized. If done properly it can elicit buyer reaction. As for No. 4, it isn't always advisable to ask for the order, but at this point in the interview it seems proper to at least put out a feeler where even a little interest is shown. No. 4 is in order.

Example No. 3. Interpretation of buyer reaction is the real skill of perception. What you have to sell will benefit the buyer and his company in increased sales, greater consumer satisfaction, more repeat orders and more profits. All you are trying to do is help him. If he doesn't give you a favorable reaction quite soon in the interview, there must be a reason.

1. Is he listening? Are you holding his interest?
2. Does he understand? Are you explaining clearly enough?
3. Is there a conflict of interest such as loyalty to another line?
4. Is there a credit problem? Franchise problem?
5. Are you using the right selling appeals for him?

Fit the following buyer reactions to the above reasons:

a. Buyer yawns. Lights a cigarette. Leans back in a relaxed way. _____

b. Buyer shows impatience. Drums on the desk. Seems a little nervous. _____

c. Buyer says, "I've got enough lines already. I can't handle them all." _____

d. Buyer says, "The time has come when I've got to clean house around here but I can't see your deal as a solution to my problem." _____

e. Buyer says, "I've made a lot of money with your competitor's line and my customers are used to it. Don't see how I could change now." _____

Answers and explanations:

a. (1) The buyer is bored and he's going to be mighty hard to sell. He's already closed off the sale in his own mind. You will have to use strong statements that you can back up such as, "The opportunity of a new dealership on our line is really a rare thing. I wouldn't want you to pass up the big sales and profits it offers because of my short-comings. Let me express it this way. . . ."

b. (2) The buyer has missed several of your points and you have gone past him. He is not hearing anything you say. He certainly won't admit it. Your only hope is to say, "Let me summarize briefly and review the advantages I can offer you one by one." If the buyer perks up a bit your perception is correct and you've got another chance —be clear this time.

c. (4) Buyer isn't showing loyalty. He's probably got too many lines and not enough good ones. He has an investment problem, isn't making money, and possibly his credit is suffering. Your solution would be to face facts with, "Frankly, I can't see how you can really make money with your investment spread. If I'm going to be of help to you let me suggest. . . ."

d. (5) This buyer wants to make a change and has no loyalty to his present lines but doesn't see your line as a solution. In order to find the right appeals you might have to probe deeper into his problem. "Your comment interests me because we have been the answer to the increased dollar sales and profits in our industry. What would you like a line to do for you that you don't think our line can do?"

e. (3) Here's a buyer who has a false sense of loyalty to an undeserving line. He knows he has to change but he keeps telling himself to put it off. You have to express a sense of urgency. "The biggest season of the year is coming up right now. If you miss it with our line now, you'll hurt your whole year's business. Let me review why you should make a change and do it today."

Continue to work on your inventory of Perception Skills as you follow your usual work patterns. You will soon be able to determine how perceptive you are and how much more practice you need in this important segment of Ingenious Selling. In the next chapter we shall take all of the natural skills, including perception, and exploit them further.

8

How to Improve and Exploit Your Skills in Directed Conversation, Persuasion, Perception, and the Three Basic Senses for Greater Daily Results

What does the expression "a born salesman" really mean? The common interpretation is that a successful salesman just doesn't have to do anything to be successful. It just happens somehow. And why not? He has a natural talent for it.

Of course, this is rubbish. If nothing else, a successful salesman has long hours of hard work to his credit. The facts are, however, that the successful salesman has studied, worked, schemed, planned, organized, and applied his skills. He has practiced and rehearsed, worked on his attitude, exploited his talents.

Great musicians have boundless musical talent, but they all have had to learn notes, dexterity with their instruments, the meaning of music as an expression, and practice fourteen hours a day—day after day, week after week. Most salesmen have great talent for the profession. They wouldn't even be in it without a talent inclination. Unfortunately, only a few really try to develop their sales skills and abilities.

The ingenious salesman must really exploit his talents. He requires more than just being a "good" salesman. He wants to be an outstanding salesman and he can live up to his own expectations. Let us explore the natural skills that lend themselves to ingenious selling, first to determine how to develop them and finally how to apply them.

What Are the Natural Skills?

1. The first of these natural selling skills is the art of directed conversation. Conversation itself is simply discourse between two or more people. Directed conversation still involves the discourse but keeps it on a guided track and manipulates it to suit a purpose. Directed conversation may be quite simple, pleasant and meaningful, and it should always be under control. It is not contrived or clever conversational fencing, nor is it intended to confound the buyer. It is a direct means to an end. It is a skill that can be developed and used for greater day-to-day results.

2. The next in order of selling skills is persuasion. Oddly enough, persuasion isn't something injected into the sales conversation. It *is* the sales conversation, part and parcel. The whole direction of the sales interview is persuasion. Persuasion is a combination of words, expressions, mannerisms, gestures, demeanor, attitude and even procedure. It is one hundred per cent developed ability.

3. Following persuasion comes perception. This is a skill that can be developed and has top priority in the successful sale. Perception is simply the ability to grasp quickly what to say, what to do, what direction to take, how to act. Good perception avoids losing sales, and creates bigger ones.

4. A new element to the natural skills is a sub-skill known as the *sense of timing*. Sometimes you know when to see the buyer and when not to—when to ask for the order and when to wait (for the yes answer). At other times you must perceive (there's that word perception

again) when and when not to act, which can only be judged by using a good sense of timing.

5. Another important sub-skill for ingenious selling is the *sense of drama*. Every sale has its element of the dramatic. Ever hear of a dramatic entrance? Think an ingenious salesman doesn't use it when he can? A portfolio presentation lends itself to drama. Drama makes the sale interesting—there is a plot and a moral, and the moral is always that the right thing to do is to take the salesman's advice.

6. Finally, we shall examine a third sub-skill, the *sense of understanding people*. Don't forget all you have learned from the old selling texts about "sizing up the buyer" because almost everything written or said is a part of understanding people. There are some new rules to go by and there is a quick way of getting to know quite a bit about a person you will engage in sales conversation. It is obvious, of course, that the better you know and understand your prospect the better sales opportunity you will have.

The aptitude which each of us has for all of these six great selling aids is talent, and the manner in which we apply them is skill. Our personal inventory in a previous chapter gave us an insight into our current abilities to use these selling skills, so now let us learn how to sharpen them for greater results through ingenious selling.

Directed Conversation

Following a sales meeting, did you ever sit around in a hotel room with a group of fellow salesmen, swapping stories and just talking? You will always find one fellow who tells a better story, holds attention, and seems most interesting without either hogging the conversation or trying to get the spotlight turned on him. He is easy and natural without effort, he doesn't interrupt (at least obviously) and when he opens his mouth he says something. He shows interest in others and asks questions (and listens to the answers).

Here is a leader, born of confidence in his skill of directed conversation. He should be the most successful salesman in the room, all other attributes being equal. Oddly enough, everyone in the room could be quite adept at conversation and even then one would stand out. This, of course, is lesson number one: no matter if there are two, five or ten in a group, there is always a leader. In a sales interview, either with a buyer alone or with the merchandise manager present, that leader must be you. Only with your skill at directed conversation can you attain that leadership quickly and hold it throughout the interview. Following are five clues to make your selling conversation sparkle.

Clue No. 1—practice summarizing.

A sales conversation is necessarily quite short. Points must be made and understood and each point must relate to the others. They must lead to a conclusion—a positive conclusion. To determine how adept you are at extemporaneous presentation, try to practice summarizing. Summarize a book you have read, a movie or TV drama that you have seen, an article you have read. *Example:*

> *The Caine Mutiny* is an absorbing story depicting the life and times of a young naval officer in World War II. Following college he joins the Navy and comes under the command of an unbalanced captain. The captain's suspicious nature and cowardice come to a climax during a hurricane when another officer forcibly takes command. Close friendships vanish when the captain is revealed to be a tragic figure during court-martial. The mutiny is vindicated but the victory is hollow. The book holds a deep and poignant lesson in human behavior.

Now practice a one-paragraph book or a movie review aloud. You won't do it well the first time or even the second time, but on the third or fourth try, things will begin to fall into place. Try again with another subject and still another. Engage your wife or luncheon friends with, "You know, Emily, I read an in-

teresting article about dentists that purported to show that. . . ."
"Charlie, I can't agree with that. *The Wall Street Journal* reported that the steel industry has taken the stand that. . . ."

We are not implying here that we make a few summaries and stop. This is something we will be conscious of for weeks—even months. However, one summary that we will work on right now is the sales presentation. The object is to know our subject cold and, under ideal practice conditions, tell an interesting and persuasive sales story and reach a buying conclusion.

Clue No. 2—head for a target.

In sales conversation the purpose is to make the sale. Now this may take the form of asking for an order, asking for display position on the counter, holding a training meeting with retail sales people, getting a co-op advertisement, a Main Street window display, even getting an audience with the president of the store. All of these things and many more lead to doing more business and they all require the successful completion of a sale of one kind or another.

So, it is imperative that we know what the target is and vary our directed conversation accordingly. Because of time limitations, it is usually wise to reveal the target early and get some kind of agreement that this is an important subject to discuss. "Mr. Williams, the purpose of my visit today is to chat with you a few minutes about a slightly different program which is bound to get more business for you. I have worked this program with good success. It involves your taking advantage of a new trend—the tremendous interest in men's toiletries." Here you have put the buyer at ease (a chat) and introduced what promises to be an interesting conversation with more sales and profits involved. What buyer wouldn't be glad to join in?

Clue No. 3—invite comment.

This is a conversation and not a speech. The normal reaction to a sales presentation is that the salesman does all the talking and the buyer gives rapt attention. The fact is the buyer quits listening after a few sentences and a point is made. The only way to get the buyer back on the track and go forward is to evoke a comment or invite some minor action. "Teen-age boys of 15-16 are luxury toiletries users to a big extent already. I expect your son has the bug, or does he?" Or, "I think if you move a little to the left you can get a better view of this display."

If you see the buyer wants to interrupt let him do it—he is showing interest and that is desirable. When you have a point half made, it is natural for you to want him to withhold comment until you are through, but suppress that impulse! He may be well ahead of you and if you can re-comment—"Exactly!"— you've got it made.

In any sales conversation it is understood that the buyer is there to listen and you are there to talk. This will always be true. Nevertheless, in ingenious selling the sales interview must be considered a discussion between salesman and buyer on the overall subject of how, together, you can make his business better. This is interesting conversational material.

Incidentally, asking and answering questions will be a separate subject in a later chapter.

Clue No. 4—keep on track.

In social conversation one subject leads to another and someone always gets the subject changed. If you are a part of that conversation and you haven't finished making your point, you quickly interject to get back to the original thought. In selling conversation you must be particularly watchful of this. The buyer is indicating a lack of interest when he changes the subject—or he doesn't understand. While you don't want to be curt, neither of you can afford the time to go off on a tangent.

The simplest method to stay on track is by use of agreement. Here's how:

The buyer is invited to comment—or simply interjects. After a few moments, you determine (by perception) either that (a) he doesn't understand, (b) he is deliberately trying to change the subject, or (c) he is still on the subject but going off on a tangent. You follow for another moment or two until you can interject the words, "Exactly, and. . . ." "You're right, and. . . ." "Yes, indeed, and. . . ." "I certainly agree, and. . . ."

A person will only let you interrupt their train of thought gracefully if you appear to be carrying it forward—that is, by agreement. Whether or not you really agree is beside the point. You must get back on track and you take the subject from the buyer's point to your own. The buyer has participated and you want him to—in fact, you'll invite him to do it again. Meanwhile, you have a good insight into his thinking and how the interview is proceeding.

Clue No. 5—inject you.

Ingenious selling requires your own personality, your opinions, your ideas, to shine through. You are the buyer's broker, insurance agent, doctor, lawyer, and pastor for the business at hand. He has to feel confidence in you as a business counselor. The company you represent and the products and program you present are only the vehicles for sales and profits. Why he uses them and how he uses them are determined by how well he accepts you as a person.

Be natural. Treat the buyer as a good (not close) friend. Be helpful and sincere. Don't worry about being a tower of strength or of being something you are not. You don't have to try to be anything other than yourself. You have a mission to perform but you are prepared, and you have confidence in your ability to make yourself understood. After all, your objective is one of mutual benefit.

As we've said before, many salesmen who are interesting in private life are lackluster in professional life. This is because they are trying to create an unreal image and it isn't coming off. When you direct a sales conversation you can activate all of the clues we have outlined to obtain a favorable result without indulging in heroics. Besides, the buyer doesn't want you to be the hero—he wants the credit—and he has reserved the champion medal for himself. And here's news—he deserves it because he makes the decision and the results are his responsibility.

We've taken our conversational inventory and now we have looked a little deeper into the directed sales conversation—an important key to ingenious selling success.

Persuasion

There are two principal secrets in mastering the skill of successful persuasion. They are:

1. Appeal to the self interest of your customer as a person.
2. Be so logical that there seems no other method of accomplishment.

The con-artist appeals to greed—get rich quick. This is pure unadulterated self-interest. And he makes it all so logical that the "mark" goes along willingly. Think of how successful these operators could be if they were sincerely trying to help people in a legitimate manner! We'll leave that to the criminologist, however. The point is that no one, no matter how altruistic, can avoid self-interest being a first consideration. Certainly, "What's good for the company is good for me" or, "What's right for the family is right for me"—and that's just the point.

The buyer must make the right decision because it is expected of him. The majority of his decisions had better be right. You can help him—and the great thing about it is that your proposition will work if you sell it right. It can't fail, and that's what ingenious selling is all about.

The first step is to treat your proposition as if it were the opportunity of a lifetime for the buyer. He has been waiting for years for circumstances to fall into place as they do right now. He can make something happen to improve the fortunes of his company—and he's bound to get credit for it. Now all of this is already understood, but to sharpen the persuasion factor of the sales conversation you slant your comments in this direction.

You mention a past success of his with your line or with some noncompetitive line. You compliment him on a current success. Then you explain how the present market situation is wide open for your new offer. This has the effect of putting the buyer into the decision on a personal basis without actually saying it. At the same time, it is all just a part of the sales conversation.

Now, this matter of being logical is the greatest secret of persuasion. And this is not too easy to explain. The fact is, you must make your proposition logical enough for the buyer to understand it fully and act on it properly—and believe in it implicitly. If he understands it, acts on it and believes in it, he *will* make it work for him—and, obviously, for you.

All selling points must be in the proper order and each point must be believable to build on the next. Now, you first examine your proposition to see how logical you can make it sound in a practice presentation. As you make each point, ask yourself, "Is it believable?" "How believable?" If your answer is questionable you must find a way to strengthen the point. Remember now, there is nothing dishonest in practicing logic to persuade a buyer to do something that will work positively if he too believes it.

As defined, logic is the science of valid and accurate thinking, the science or art of reasoning, a right use of thought or the rational powers. The way it is used is a comparative thing. Something is right because something else is right. *For example:*

1. People have more discretionary income today than ever before; *therefore,* there will be more spending for things that were once considered luxuries. This has happened before and so it is *assumed* that it will happen again.
2. A teen-age fad is prevalent in New York, Los Angeles, and Chicago; *therefore,* it will become prevalent in St. Louis. This has happened before so it is *assumed* that it will happen again.
3. Two years ago a store sold forty gross of a men's grooming aid in a two-week period of its promotional introduction. Since then, the total business of the store has doubled. It is, therefore, logical to assume that on the present introduction of a new men's grooming aid sales can reasonably be expected to reach sixty gross.

The directed sales conversation should be sprinkled with buyer self-interest and loaded with logic. Obviously, it must be expressed and organized well. These, then, are the keys to persuasive strength for any ingenious salesman.

Perception

Perception is one of those talents of which it is said, "Either you have it or you don't and if you don't, forget it." The fact is, however, a person can become perceptive within a narrow range just by long experience. Older, more experienced salesmen are as a rule more perceptive in the profession than the "few years" veteran. This is because they know what to look for —what to expect. Had they the clues to developing this talent, they would have become even more proficient over the years.

Perception can be described as insight or comprehension, discernment, or discrimination. In a sales sense it is the ability to judge how the buyer is reacting to the sales presentation, the ability to discern the buyer's innermost feelings. Once these are perceived, so to speak, it is possible to proceed with the sales conversation toward a more certain result. Let's look at some examples—during the sales interview they might take the form of questions to yourself:

1. I wonder what the buyer's reaction is to my product line as compared to my competitor's?
2. Is he understanding? Am I taking enough time? If I move faster, will he follow?
3. Am I getting agreement? Is it time to close? Can I now assume that he is favorably inclined?

These and many other questions to yourself fairly deluge your thinking as you engage in directed sales conversation. They are automatic; you simply can't help them. However, your answers to yourself, which are also automatic, may be mostly right or mostly wrong. These answers obviously determine how perceptive you are. And—this is something that can be developed.

There is one big clue to good perception—*learn to think like a buyer*. However, as the cornball puts it, "This is easier said than done." Yet without knowing it, this is the way the older salesmen learned how to be perceptive and use this talent to garner more orders, bigger orders, retrieve lost sales, operate more efficiently.

Now, the buyer will give an outward appearance of how he is thinking by what he says and how he acts. But you can't depend upon that. Too often you end up by asking yourself, "What could have gone wrong? He seemed to be going along with me all the way and just when things looked best he suddenly changed." The fact is he didn't change at all. He never was "going along." He just talked and acted that way. If you had perceived his true feelings you could have regrouped and saved the sale.

How do you learn to think like a buyer? Well, the *first way* is by being one on your off hours—every time you shop for anything. For example: You have a favorite brand of toothpaste. Next time you shop, tell the clerk that you're getting weary of the brand (which you are not) and ask for a recommendation. Listen attentively to what the clerk tells you about another brand. As you walk out with your favorite brand recall your reaction to the clerk's "pitch." Why couldn't you be sold?

Keep in mind that any buyer is suspicious of change—and that includes you when you're a buyer—and even though there is an appearance of agreement, it may not be there. This is particularly so when it involves change. Look for clues to perceive agreement when you are recommending change.

The *second way* to learn to think like a buyer is to ask the buyer for advice:

> Charlie, you and I have been in this business several years now, each of us in a different capacity, and I've always respected your opinion from your bird's-eye view. What do you think of . . . . ?

Remember now, *don't* ask about the proposition you are selling during this interview. This is not a sales approach as used in this instance. What you are trying to do here is get a line on the buyer's reactions.

This is too blunt an approach for exposure of the present offer. You might get a quick "no" for an answer. It is even best that this line of questioning follow completion of a successful sale when the buyer is relaxed and can express an honest opinion.

The questions may be on national advertising, value of clerk support at the counter, consumer response to retailer promotion or many of the dozens of other things that relate to your business but are not directly concerned with the issue at hand. You can pick up some valuable reactions that can help your future perception skills.

A *third method* is to review each of your sales interviews mentally, immediately after each interview, and determine where the tide turned into either failure or success. You will recall the sales situation as it existed and with it you will perceive the buyer's reaction. Now that you know the reaction ask yourself, "If I were in the buyer's shoes, honestly now, what would my reaction have been?"

Many salesmen are loath to give two minutes following an interview to a mental review of the interview's events. They would rather wait until later—and then they usually procrastinate again. But this two minutes can be so valuable that you should train yourself to do it. You can spot reasons for success or failure and at the same time give yourself valuable lessons in perception by learning to think like a buyer.

Perception is a hidden talent that can be developed if one is aware that skill in its use can be very valuable in determining sales results. Yet, you hardly need be conscious of it during a sales conversation. Rightly or wrongly, you will judge the buyer's reaction and take steps accordingly. If you understand how the buyer thinks and think like him, you'll be able to make more right decisions than wrong ones for greater selling success.

The Sub-Skill Senses—Timing, Drama, Understanding

We have identified directed conversation, persuasion and perception as three skills of ingenious selling, all of which require certain methods for development. Now, we shall investigate the three senses that require more mechanical treatment for making them useful skills in the ingenious sales kit.

Let's consider the sense of timing first

Scheduling the sales interview in the first place requires timing. Is it the right season? Too soon? Too late? Would the buyer normally make a decision at this time? Suppose the buyer usually plays golf on Wednesday afternoon but will stay for an hour or so for a salesman with an important message—and you wander in at twelve noon? Is your subject going to get favorable attention under these circumstances? You have to decide things like this and sometimes quickly.

Timing, however, in the sense we want to discuss it here, relates to the directed sales conversation itself: (a) When do I go on to the next point? (b) Should I now put out my first feeler for the order? There are dozens of these decisions to be made during the interview and a good sales sense of timing enables the right decision at the right time.

Don't confuse timing with perception. The clue to good timing is the direct question. A good sense of timing is necessary to know where and when to place the question.

1. You begin the conversation with what seems to you an interesting and provocative subject. You get little buyer reaction. You say, "From your sales and profit interests this seems a timely subject, don't you think?"
2. You continue and soon want to move on to the next point. You say, "Before I move into another consideration, let me ask you if you feel that the last points were well taken? They are the crux of this whole interview. What do you think?"
3. You move into the close and begin asking for "yes" answers. "I think you would agree that . . . , wouldn't you?" If you get a negative reaction, you say, "Well, at least you would agree that . . . , right?"

There is a good deal of intuition in timing. You sense from how the interview is going that now is the time to make a certain point. In ingenious selling, the selling interview and the conversation surrounding it are so well planned that intuitive timing becomes natural. Sometimes the conversation simply prompts the buyer into leading the sale until asking for the order is automatic. Here is an illustration:

> In New York City, there are several buildings whose business tenants have large display rooms catering to the "gift" store retail trade. They feature imports and unusual items of many descriptions: Art carvings, paintings, antique-type gifts and on and on.
> A cardinal principle of the floor salesman is to simply let the retail buyer browse and stand by to answer questions. The questions change from, "How is this made?" and, "What is this material?" to, "How does this sell?" and, "What shops are buying this?" The prospective buyer has seen all he wants to and is faced with making a decision—whether to leave or to begin buying.
> The salesman must sense this moment intuitively and engage the buyer in conversation on an item for which special interest was shown. "Mr. Customer, you took an interest in that Grecian Urn. You're from Ohio and I have a customer from Hamilton, Ohio, who selected that piece over a year ago and he has re-ordered good quantities four times since then." The salesman could have made that statement when the prospect was looking at the item but the timing wasn't right. Now he uses it to lead to the order when the dealer is ready to buy.

Develop your sense of timing by asking questions, by relying on intuition and by learning patience in holding your strong points for your presentation, when they count the most. We shall discuss the planned sale in depth in a following chapter.

What is the sense of drama?

All life is a play, all people the players. Almost everyone loves a good show, even buyers. A feeling for the dramatic is a real asset in making a successful sale. It is a necessity for the ingenious salesman. Now, we're not advocating playing a part but, rather, living the part. We are not recommending Shakespearean tactics (or antics) or anything of that nature. We are advising using dramatics to make strong impressions.

The clues to a sense of the dramatic are seriousness and sincerity. *Example:* You have been conducting an interesting conversation and have led to a conclusion. The air has been light and with a sprinkle of humor. Suddenly you grow serious, and with obvious sincerity you say, "You know, Sam, there's no other way you can get the sales and profits out of this business except with our line—if you use it right. I've proved it with others and I can prove it with you. That's all I'm trying to do—just help you get more of what's yours." Then you come with a quip, "All that I am or ever hope to be, I owe to helping others get what belongs to them already." Your customer gets the point.

Directed sales conversation is light and witty, concise and accurate. You steer the buyer off the unpleasant and toward the objective, and when you must make an impression you use dramatics. It will then be remembered and will provide the emotional influence that leads to the sale.

How to develop the sense of understanding people

Selling is an individual matter and requires a better understanding of how people are going to react than do other professions. Selling necessitates a face-to-face human situation and a mishandling means sure disaster, at least so far as that particular sale is concerned. Most writers on selling like to "type" buyers into women buyers, angry buyers, silent buyers, and others. That's all right so far as suggestions on handling are concerned; in fact, we'll discuss it later. However, you simply can't understand people by typing them.

Things that would be helpful to know about your buyer might include these: Does he have a sense of humor? What kind—a sense of the ridiculous? Slapstick? Is he a happy person? A born critic? Suspicious? Gullible? Pessimistic? Optimistic? These characteristic human elements all take their part in the selling interview.

Knowing that the buyer is a fisherman, golfer, hunter, boating enthusiast, good family man, woman chaser, drinker or non-drinker may be helpful in a way, but don't mistake these things for understanding. In fact, be careful of diversionary subjects. Anyway you look at it, the reason you came in was to talk business. These hobbies and surface diversions are the things that you can find out from others—salesmen, clerks, acquaintances. The really helpful information about your buyer you are going to have to find out for yourself. Of course, the longer you do business with a buyer the better you know him (or think you do), and sometimes even this can be a handicap. The best attitude for you to take is friendly and businesslike. But it is necessary to get a feel for those innermost characteristics that make him tick.

On a first meeting be serious and cordial. "Mr. Wilson, I've only been in *this* territory a short time and I've looked forward to our meeting because it's evident that you people are good merchandisers." Does he seem a little pleased? Let's try a wee bit of humor. "But why take only the lion's share of your market when you can get it all?" He smiles and makes a comment which lets you believe that you can be light without his thinking you flippant. You continue, "You can literally get the whole share of the ——— market with this line, Mr. Wilson, and I'll show you how." The telephone rings and he talks for less than a minute, answers a question positively and hangs up. He is a man of decision.

"Here are the four basic uses for our product—and the quality benefits the customer wants. We have them all, plus these additional benefits our competitors don't have." An associate stops by to ask him to play golf tomorrow; he seems to want to play but replies that it looks like rain and that he'll call him tonight. A little pessimistic? You say, "I think you'll agree that these are worthwhile consumer benefits, especially this (the strongest), wouldn't you?" He replies positively but indicates that they have done well with your competitor for the last several years. Too critical? Well, no—he's bound to put up some defense.

Well, that's far enough to illustrate the point: The clue to understanding your buyer is to learn as you go along in the interview—and be conscious of what you learn. Of course, it doesn't do you much good if, after you're on the street without a sale, you say to yourself, "Yeah, but I sure understand that buyer!" You also *use* what you learn as you go along with the interview. You're not there trying to hire an assistant—you're trying to make a sale.

We shall call this the "inquisitive" type of directed sales conversation. You can become so adept at it that within three months you'll know much more about how to treat your individual buyers—and you'll feel that new buyers are old friends. There is a little trick to this kind of sales conversation but you won't feel awkward with it at any time, and it's really only a matter of concentration during the whole interview.

There definitely is a secret to understanding the people you do business with and that secret is that no one else can do your research for you. But you can "learn as you earn" and what you learn on your own is what makes up that essential asset we call experience.

In this chapter we've examined three natural skills—conversation, persuasion, and perception—and our application of them; and three sub-skills—the sense of timing, dramatics, and understanding buyers—and our use of them. All of these are vital to the concept of ingenious selling. Now we shall move ahead to solving selling problems via the use of ingenious methods.

9

New and Ingenious Approaches for Translating Major Selling Problems Into Personal Sales Opportunities

In the next four chapters we will provide direction to your selling effort by outlining ingenious means of applying your newly learned techniques. This is where the fun of selling makes its appearance—and the joys of accomplishment.

If you have merely read this book to this point and have given thought to what you have read, you are already on your way to becoming a more successful salesman. You can't miss because thinking about your selling assignment with this new approach to improvement will make your day-to-day experiences more meaningful and, therefore, more productive.

On the other hand, if you have studied this book and worked diligently on it, you are on the road to becoming an outstanding salesman in your field because you are learning how to become ingenious. You will be infinitely better organized to be at the right place at the right time and you will be better prepared to make the most of your efforts. Your sales interviews will turn out well as a result of better application of your skills in persuasion and perception and also as a result of your improvement in directed conversation. You will approach each selling situation with a new found confidence and positive attitude.

We have been exploring the wide avenues by which you can "learn as you earn" so to speak—and we are cognizant that selling is a profession that cannot be catalogued. At this juncture, however, we will, by illustration and example, take the more common selling problems and work out ingenious selling solutions. Even though you will employ your own "on the spot" solutions, these examples will provide direction and some valuable tips on procedure. You should enjoy it.

How to Work with Your Supervisor

When you first learn that your supervisor is coming to work with you, ask these questions of yourself:

1. Why is he coming to work with me? Has my performance been below par? Is this simply a routine supervisory visit? Could there be some ulterior motive?
2. What will he want to do? Where will he want to go? How will he want to handle the selling interviews and situations?
3. What can I accomplish with his visit? How can I make the best use of his time and talent? How can I display my own abilities in the best light?

The first two sets of questions are quite difficult to answer if the supervisor appears on the scene rarely or if this is among his first few visits. In other words, after you know your supervisor better it is easier to anticipate his reasons for coming and the plans for his trip. For the purpose of this examination, we will assume that your supervisor has worked with you on several previous occasions and does make a fairly regular appearance. In any case, you will want to ask and answer the questions anyway.

Question 1.
Why is he coming to work with me? Has my performance been below par? Is this simply a routine supervisory visit? Could there be some ulterior motive?

Answer 1.
If your performance is below par, even if the supervisor visits you regularly, you can be certain he will hit on your weak spots.

Know what they are and ask him for help on them before he can bring them up to you. You must take the initiative. Remember that even if he didn't come with this purpose in mind *this is where you need help.* You do not put him on the defensive but rather in a position where much can be accomplished and his image of you goes up a notch.

If your performance appears satisfactory and if the supervisor makes routine visits, even then determine your most vulnerable spots and get them into the open. Here are some examples:

a. Have you been able to hit what you consider a satisfactory daily call average? What can he do to help you improve your routing patterns? How can he help you get better organized? How can you reduce your per call time with better results?

b. How about orders to calls? Do you have inventory problems in some products which keep you from getting orders on other products? Can he help you with exchanges through the home office?

c. If you are not doing well on certain offers or promotions, what are others doing who are successful? How can he help you with any additional support through headquarters?

It is wise in some cases where you have advance notice of your supervisor's visit to drop him a note telling him you will welcome him because of certain problems—and outline them. In this way, you are setting the tenor of his call so as to be of the most value to you.

In any event, the first step is always to establish concretely why he came. "Charlie," you say, "I'm really glad to see you because I have a few problems I believe you can help me solve." You name them. "Now if you'll tell me what you have on your mind we can plan our work."

You have assumed the initiative. The supervisor expects you to do this.

Question 2.

What will he want to do? Where will he want to go? How will he want to handle the selling interviews and situations?

Answer 2.

Before the supervisor arrives you will have two schedules ready. Both the first plan and the alternate will be aimed to cover the problems you want solved. You will have a time and routing schedule, the names of the accounts you will see and what you hope to accomplish in each account *with his help.*

Whatever you plan, make your supervisor a part of it. In this regard you will want to be completely cooperative. A good method is to share the responsibility for the success of the sale. The analysis later should be on a "we" basis. "We should have done that," or "We should not have done this."

After your supervisor arrives and has expressed himself on the purpose of his visit, you will want to nail down how you expect it to be accomplished. "Well," you say, "in keeping with getting my problems solved, I had two plans of procedure. . . . However, your objectives have altered them a bit so I suggest we. . . ." Although your supervisor may be a bit suspicious of your "taking over," he will expect any strong salesman to do that.

Your time is valuable and the worst attitude you can take is, "My time is your time and anything you want to do is all right with me." Better that he feel that you know why he is there, what he expects to accomplish and that you have planned a productive way to get it done. Daylight hours are for calls. After hours are for records and organization.

If you have any control over arrival time and length of visit, keep in mind that you should have an introductory, planning, and organizing period, one full working day, and a review and conclusions period. It is well if your supervisor should arrive early in the evening prior to the work day for the planning session. You can then work all of the next day and have a review session the same evening.

Even though the supervisor wants only to make one or two problem calls with you, he will not know how you work and will not be of real help unless he spends a full working day. He has a time problem too, but your productive time is actually more valuable to him and to the company than his own. He can afford to make concessions with it more than you can.

Question 3.

What can I accomplish with his visit? How can I make the best use of his time and talent? How can I display my own abilities in the best light?

Answer 3.

Working with your supervisor will slow you up a little but in most cases can be more productive than working alone. It is often said that most accounts do not like to give orders when the salesman is working with someone. Don't you believe it. Most accounts don't want to buy—period. In fact, they are usually flattered (if you help to make it so) when a home office supervisor calls on them. Nevertheless, plan the day about one call shorter than usual—and so inform your supervisor.

More than likely, the supervisor will want to visit certain key accounts—this is O.K. but try to steer him into accounts where he can do you some good. At the same time, try to follow as much of your usual routine as you can. Even take the supervisor in on detail and policing calls if you can. You want him to know your usual pattern and how well you cover and control your accounts.

You can't be certain it will work out this way but, unless you have a very special problem your supervisor should not take over the call. He will be expected to add to the sales conversation and should supplement your remarks. He should answer all questions addressed to him and not those addressed to you. Make certain that the supervisor is briefed on people and situations—it is to your advantage to make him look good.

When you enter the store begin introductions immediately. Let the supervisor help you with the inventory. Make certain he knows the size and mix of the order you are going to suggest. Make a positive introduction to the buyer. The supervisor will make a few appropriate comments, then you start the presentation: "The reason that Mr. Wilson is with me today is primarily to visit with you people. We feel that your stature in this market promises a potential for you that warrants all the help we can give you. Let me start by saying. . . ."

The delicate part of the interview is the detail of the order. You should work on detail alone with the buyer while the supervisor stands by. If this is not followed, the buyer often feels you are "ganging up on him." You should be in control when the interview closes with a few constructive words from your supervisor.

Your *supervisor's objectives* in working with you are to check up on you and to make certain you get on and stay on the right track. Naturally, he wants his own reflection of the company to look good in the process. You can only gain through complete cooperation with him.

Your objectives are, first, to accomplish a good selling day and to pick up valuable pointers. Next, to reflect your image in the best light possible. Don't indulge in excuses—and see to it that your supervisor views your selling situation as you view it.

How to Control the Big Territory

Every territory is different in make-up and complexity. All have their special problems. The big territory as we define it here is the territory with many, many customers, large and small. It may cover a fairly big geographical area or a relatively little one.

In such a territory, there are some accounts that require a visit once a month, others once a quarter, still others twice a year and many not at all—the wholesaler's salesman contacts these latter accounts. The obvious problem of the big territory is the retail account's lethargy in keeping up displays and the effort on your line between your infrequent calls. You can't get around fast enough and the wholesaler's salesman has too many other things to sell and service. Meanwhile, your competition always seems to be undoing your efforts and doing their own faster than you can keep up.

The answer is the *policing action* and the unique application of it. Here's how it works:

1. Planning your routing to make four, five or six additional "bumble bee" calls each day—in other words, just in and out. You don't list these calls on your routing. You still make your planned calls per day and, as it is convenient for you to do so, you "drop in" to smaller accounts for the "policing action."

2. *You do not interview the "policing call" retailer.* You check the location and type of your display and its inventory condition. You note your competitor's position and inventory. You make a general appraisal of the overall store—location, traffic, appearance. All of these things you note down on a prepared form called a "Store Check."

3. You *later* visit with the sales managers of the *various* (possibly two or three) wholesalers who service this area and discuss with *each* of them the conditions you have found. You pinpoint the responsibility to the wholesale salesman for each retail account involved. Note: As you have not asked the retailer what wholesaler services his account, you do advise and alert *each wholesaler* about the conditions you found. In this manner, you can get pressure on the retail account for your line *by inviting competition on your products* at the wholesale level.

Let's illustrate

You are selling a sundry drug product carried by all drug stores. You handle department store and supermarket drug departments direct as well as large chain drug stores. All independents and small chains are handled by drug wholesalers. Several competing drug wholesalers handle your line in each area. You do a considerable amount of turnover order work (detailing) among the better independent drug stores for your wholesalers. However, there are hundreds you personally can't reach.

Each day, however, you do "look in" on a few of these stores and make out a condition (Store Check) report. This only takes a few minutes and does not slow down your regular call routine. On the occasion of your call on one of the wholesalers who service the area, you pull out the reports that apply to him. Here's what you say:

"Mr. Sales Manager, which of your salesmen calls on West End Drug at 10th and Western? Please tell him to check my display right away—and do it regularly after this. The display is nearly empty and it's been moved to a back bar. Look, I can't be turning orders for better accounts if you don't back me up in these other stores. If I have to check that store again I'll have to sell them myself and turn the order to a wholesaler who will keep my display in order and in stock."

If you don't know the wholesaler in question, you give the story to competing area wholesalers in the same manner. The wholesaler who has the business will want to keep it—the wholesalers who do not have the business will want to get it. The competition will impress the retailer with the importance of your line. Keep this up day in and day out and your products will get more and better attention all the time. Remember, however, do *not* switch wholesalers for an account without thorough discussion with the wholesaler beforehand. The existing wholesaler should be given every opportunity to retain the business.

The wholesalers involved also should know you are taking this approach. This is no popularity contest. Win your wholesale customer's respect and you win his support.

The Buying Committee

Most larger chain organizations, chain drug stores, discount department stores, food and household item supermarkets, operate through buying committees. The function of these buying committees varies greatly from organization to organization. Some buying committees concentrate on new products, new items and new lines almost exclusively. Others include new offers on established lines. Still others decide on products and lines, from among those carried, to push on seasonal promotions such as "back to school" or Christmas.

In every case, the buying committee is all powerful. In most cases, the salesman does not know the extent of the authority of the buying committee or, in many cases, even if there is one. A rule of thumb is that where an immediate buying decision is not made by the buyer—either yes or no—a buying committee is involved. In one or two calls the salesman can determine quite accurately the buying committee's authority.

For those accounts who work through a buying committee,

the work of the salesman is imperative. The approach to the buyer must be different because the buyer in turn presents your offer to the committee—emotion free. He must be factual and analytical. Oftentimes, he must present your competitor's offer at the same time for comparison. He must be brief and to the point and sometimes he is not permitted to express an opinion.

It is the job of the salesman to prepare the buyer for all of these eventualities in the following order:

1. The salesman must first "sell" the buyer on the proposition so he will take it to the committee. The buyer is expected to "weed out" all those things which he thinks the committee would not consider. If he brings a lot of irrelevant matters to the committee's attention, he will be accused of poor judgment.
2. The salesman must equip the buyer with factual material in written, easy-to-understand form to present to the buying committee. The material must be brief, points clear and concise, the sequence logical.
3. The salesman must train the buyer (without the buyer realizing it) to present his case in a way that will cause the buying committee to give it approval.
4. The salesman should persuade the buyer to present his offer rather than his competitor's and if he can't do that, he must prepare him so strongly that the competitor's offer looks weak by comparison.
5. The salesman must provide excitement by *predicting results* in a dramatic manner. This provides the emotionalism which influences the committee's agreement, whether the salesman is present or not.

Let's work out a check list on how all these things are accomplished:

1. You make up a portfolio of the offer. Get 8½ x 11 outside cover material from a stationery store (not ring binder) and personalize the outside cover with a label such as: "A back to school promotion for H. J. Wilson and Sons to increase leather goods and luggage business 20 per cent for the period."

a. On page one, you have a couple of statistics to show how industry sales are up during August and September. You show how sales of your products are ahead of the industry because your line lends itself to this market. You show that consumers' interest in your line at this time is so strong that if the stores promote it, they will invite customers who will *also* buy other school products. Use an outstanding example if possible.

b. On page two, show how your company recognizes this opportunity and what your company is doing about it. Show your company's advertising and explain the promotion. Have an illustration of your display offer. Explain the merchandise assortment —*why* a "heavy up" in certain items.

c. On page three, tell what the store is to do, i.e., (1) Clerks all wear buttons saying, "Ask me how to save 20 per cent on school luggage," (2) Co-op advertising and explain details, (3) Window display, (4) Counter display, (5) Clerk incentive program, (6) Store door coupon handout, etc. Make these things graphic enough so that the committee can actually see customers selecting luggage items.

d. On page four, predict results—specifically. For example: "This is the second year of promoting this line in the Wilson stores. Following is a list of item sales August and September last year and objective sales this year with this promotion:

Item No.	Sales last year		Objective this year		Increase
	No.	$	No.	$	$
#021643	11	550	20	1,000	450
#032728	16	320	20	400	80
#032730	—	—	15	450	450
etc.	—	—	—	—	—
Total	—	3,600	—	7,200	3,600
		Increase 100%			

    e. On page four, recommend warehouse back up stock and outline a time schedule on order placing and delivery dates—reorder information. Point out the urgency of early decision.

2. After your presentation book is made up, run through a practice presentation before you see the buyer—anticipate questions and answers. When you do interview the buyer, use the presentation as a guide. Try to keep your presentation as close to the way you would like him to present it to the buying committee as possible.

    Your explanation must be more detailed because you must prepare the buyer with a simple presentation to the committee. When he asks questions be certain that he understands the answers.

    Rehearse the buyer by using some statements which ho will be likely to remember in making his own presentation to the buying committee. Examples are:

    a. This line has been doing more to capture the young college market and the "jet set" than any others.
    b. This promotion is a traffic builder for the department as well as a money maker on its own.
    c. It's important for your stores to identify with a line which has appeal for young people.

    Above all, make your presentation as if it were for the ears of the buyer alone. He is jealous of his prerogatives. He wants to make the decision to take your proposition to the buying committee. Unless he intimates that he must present the offer to the committee, you must go after the order as if you could get it then and there.

3. If the buyer gives you a "no" answer it only means you have not sold him on taking your offer to the committee. Your job is not to get a "yes" answer because he can't give you a positive yes. All you need is a "maybe." That means he will at least see the committee. This is where

the "personal" appeal of your product offer becomes an important factor. You have the feeling that your presentation is strong enough to get committee approval even if the buyer doesn't give it support. This kind of direction often works: "Let's take a look at this offer in this light—the market situation couldn't be better. Your business could stand some up-grading—you've said that. Believe me, this proposition is really the only way you can get this business in volume that's important. You personally can get the credit for changing a static situation for your stores. I think you owe it to yourself, Ben, to give this more thought than just these few minutes allow—maybe even chat about it with Mr. Wilson. Keep this presentation and if there are any questions give me a call. Meanwhile, when do you want me to check back with you?"

The chances are very good that the buyer will agree to give your offer more consideration—he feels he isn't losing anything by that. However, once you leave and your presentation remains, he will feel duty bound to submit it to the buying committee. You can't ask more than that. So—who said that the emotional appeals were dead in so far as buying committee selling was concerned? If anything, there has to be more, not less, emotional factors involved in the buying committee situation.

Obviously, the buying committee cannot work without the salesman. What would they have to consider? Were they left to their own devices to locate the new products and promotional offers, they would be lost.

Moreover, the buying committee requires the services of a screening buyer but, in many cases, weakens him because of elimination of decision making on his part. The "review buying committee," i.e., one that lets the buyer make the decision which the committee "reviews," doesn't help either, because buyers often wait to make a purchase until *after* the committee makes its "review."

Under any circumstances, there's no more effective way to approach the buying committee situation than through the personal services of an ingenious individual salesman.

Computer Buying

Will the computer take the guesswork out of buying? Many super retailers think that eventually it will. Is this really a positive retail benefit? Many of the same retailers have their doubts. They feel that over-buying and "mistake" buying creates excitement opportunities for price and special promotions that in turn create store traffic and cement the store image for value.

On the other hand, computer buying on standard items tends to "free up" buyers' time for more concentration on promotional store events and new and different products. It makes a different job of buying.

It requires of suppliers a different kind of selling, too—if anything, more sales contact is required, not less. Better sales techniques in the merchandising aspects of selling are most certainly necessary.

Computer buying will become much more sophisticated as time goes on. Right now, the simplified procedure is as follows:

1. On standard items (and new products as they become standard) a controlled stock inventory is established.
2. From retail sales slips the computer keeps a perpetual inventory. (On items subject to high pilfer rates, a physical inventory is also necessary.)
3. When stock gets down to rebuy levels an automatic reorder is placed with the supplier.
4. In some cases, the supplier's computer accepts a physical retail inventory and figures out the order.

All of this is a simple explanation of what can be a rather complex procedure. Actually, we are only looking for end results so that we can illustrate the role of the salesman and explain how he can treat computer buying as an opportunity. Let's proceed with a check list.

1. It is obvious that both salesman and buyer must decide upon a stock inventory. The inventory must be large enough to offer good consumer selection and small enough for good turnover on investment. This in itself is a big problem and often requires compromise. With many products, lower turnover is offset by higher discounts and better datings. Moreover, there can be seasonal changes in inventory levels. Now, while the computer can keep track of everything, someone has to pump in information in the first place. The salesman, with his wealth of knowledge of product acceptability and turnover rates, certainly must be a part of this initial procedure.

2. Many stores (particularly department and discount stores) operate on an "open to buy" program which controls the investment in a whole department. For example, in a department store stationery department, needed writing instruments on order might have to wait for confirmation because the department is overexpended—possibly with things like ring binders, seasonally stocked for back to school. However, even this can be programmed on a computer basis. Now, a supplier's salesman should *not be misled* into thinking that because the store is in a rebuy position that he is automatically going to get an order. A salesman is required here to persuade the store management to ignore "not open to buy" in this instance—or at least get his orders top priority when "open to buy" occurs on the computer.

3. As yet, the computer has not approached the subject of what to display, where to display it, when to display it, the size, design and character of the display, how long the display stays up and how often it is restocked. These

things revolve around "people" decisions—salesmen, buyers, merchandise managers, manufacturing marketing groups.

Likewise on the matter of "in store" promotion, co-op advertising, clerk training, window display, and all traffic builders. These things yet require the reasoning abilities and experience of people—and a key person is the salesman.

The "perpetual" inventory has to be checked every so often with a physical inventory—so, we're almost right back where we started. Also, as mentioned, where pilferage is a problem a perpetual inventory from sales slips becomes useless. Actually, in some cases, the inventory can be gone completely and the computer cannot recognize it because there would be no sales slips. For products subject to variable pilferage, a "seeded" inventory system is best. To illustrate:

Suppose a product is packed in boxes of a dozen. The retailer shows three dozen on display, three dozen understock and twenty-four dozen in the warehouse. Each box of twelve is "seeded," i.e., a quantity, size, color, brand, and item ticket is affixed to the box. When an understock box is put on display the ticket is taken off and sent to the warehouse and another box is sent for understock. The computer keeps inventory on the warehouse stock only.

So—that's enough check listing. What happens—what do you do when one of your customers goes on a computer? The first thing you don't do is panic. You will not lose your customer. Why?

1. If your company doesn't have a computer program for handling standard items, it obviously can't team up with your customer. You'll be taking orders in the same way, *except* that the computer will be doing your inventory work for you.

2. If your company does have a computer program to team up with your customer, so much the better. The system will not only relieve you of inventory chores on standard items, but will write your orders on them, too. Yet you will have to be present for policing the system and taking the periodic physical inventories.

   a. You will have to adjust seasonal inventory levels—and keep up consumer selection levels.
   b. You will have to program new products for computer inventory control.
   c. Both your time and the buyer's time will be freed up to do a better merchandising and promotion job on your line.
   d. Your time will be freed up to spend more time developing new business elsewhere.
   e. In situations like this, your job is *not* to sell merchandise, anyway—it is to sell counter position for your line. And that job is the same as it always was.

3. The store will tell you that the computer will figure turnover rates, investment to sales and other things that could be detrimental to you. Still don't panic! Suppose they find that nylon stockings have better turnover and investment sales ratios than your leather products. Will they turn the whole first floor over to women's hose? Of course not!

   But if your competitor is beating you—ah!—that's another horse! You become important to figure out why: Better display? In store promotion? Advertising? Clerk support? In other words, the computer has made you more valuable than ever.

So, you can face computer buying in a cooperative way. Be helpful to your customer in setting up his system and ask him to reward you only with a guarantee of good counter position, promotional and clerk support. You can't lose.

Now at the wholesale level there's not much problem because

actually the wholesale inventory is only an extension of factory inventory anyway. If you can standardize on items, a computer system can only help you.

So far as the wholesaler is concerned, your job is presenting new programs and products, helping his sales force, conducting sales meetings, suggesting new techniques.

In any event, don't take extensive data processing courses—unless you intend to try to make a future with I.B.M. But maybe just a little layman type reading on the subject wouldn't hurt.

Let's summarize: We have analyzed and discussed:

1. Working with your supervisor. This should be viewed as an opportunity to be exploited.
2. Controlling the big territory. There are factors working for you if you harness them properly.
3. The buying committee. This is a bugaboo that can be turned into an effective asset.
4. Computer buying. Here is another goblin that turns out to be a money maker for the salesman.

Today's modern salesman is more necessary and more effective than ever—and his opportunities are boundless!

10

How You Can Turn Weak, Ineffective Interviews into Successful Ones via a Technique Of Exploiting the Unexpected

Throughout this book, we have stressed that successful selling requires completely different learning techniques as compared to other professions. At this point in the book, many of these learning techniques have already been explored and you will be using them daily with resultant day-by-day improvement in your selling performance. Now, however, ingenious selling skills face their greatest challenge—that of the most elusive and most damaging of all sales problems. . . .

The Problem of the Unexpected

Each selling interview produces the unexpected—and it is the unexpected that reduces orders and loses sales. Therefore, providing for the unexpected demands the most paramount skills of ingenious selling. That's what this chapter is all about.

Now, if something is truly unexpected it cannot be anticipated—if you anticipated it and planned for it, it wouldn't be unexpected. Or would it? In ingenious selling, it is possible to prepare in advance for a sales obstacle which might be totally unfamiliar, unknown, and unexpected. You not only can learn to cope with the unexpected but actually to exploit it for greater results.

Before we analyze and examine this important aspect of selling, let us review some examples.

1. You have an 11:15 A.M. appointment with the buyer.
   He is delayed twenty minutes to 11:35 A.M. and he
   apologizes by telling you he can only give you fifteen
   minutes (of a thirty minute appointment) because the
   president of the store wants him "in his office" promptly
   at 11:50 A.M. This is an example of the unexpected in
   the first phase of the interview, "Approaching the Selling Situation."

2. In another example, you have just opened with your
   introductory remarks to set the tenor for the interview
   and the buyer interrupts with, "Charlie, your competitor just left and he concluded with the same points you
   say you're going to prove." This is an example of the
   unexpected in the second phase of the interview, "Introduction to the Sale."

3. You are in the concluding area of your presentation
   when the telephone rings and something is said to the
   buyer that leaves him visibly shaken. This is an example of the unexpected in the third phase of the interview, "Making the Selling Presentation."

4. You are in the process of going over the inventory and
   settling the details of the order when a stock room boy
   interrupts: "Mr. Wilson, two of the branch stores called
   this morning to say that their inventories needed adjustment and said not to buy until they could get the
   situation squared away." This is an example of the unexpected in the fourth phase of the interview, "Getting
   the Order."

5. For a final example, you have completed the order and
   taken your leave of the buyer only to find your competitor has a scheduled advertising/counter promotion
   with the store and that it is due to break about the time
   your order arrives. This is an example of the unexpected

in the fifth phase of the interview, "Follow-up of the Sale."

Actually, the unexpected in any form and to any degree is bound to make an appearance in every complete sales interview. Most of the time it has a dampening effect and reduces both the size of the order and the dealer's enthusiasm. At other times, it can kill the sale dead. In fact, there is nothing more dampening and deadening than something totally unexpected.

The reason the examples above were delineated into the various steps leading toward the sale is because the only way to fight the unexpected is to break it down into the broad categories of the basic elements that make up the sale. We might determine means of making unexpected objections act as a starting point to strengthen the sale and improve the result. As we develop each step up the selling ladder, we will take a hard look at the unexpected and learn to exploit it.

How to Approach the Selling Situation

Approaching the selling situation begins with the planning of each particular sale and extends to actual confrontation with the buyer. With a manufacturer's direct representative in consumer goods on retail calls, it would include preliminary inventory and sales clerk interview as well as display arranging. On wholesale calls, it might include a preliminary interview with the wholesale sales manager before seeing the buyer.

With an insurance salesman, approaching the selling situation would involve only the planning period—individual data on the prospect and a rehearsed presentation tailored to the prospect's personal situation. With an automobile salesman, approaching the selling situation is planning, in most instances, for interviewing a prospect that is unknown. In this instance, only general preparation is possible. In both of these examples, we are dealing with direct consumer selling where the unexpected is a way of life, so to speak, in the selling procedure.

In approaching the selling situation for each individual sale, you must first tell yourself that something unusual, different, or unexpected will make its appearance during the selling inter-view—it may be major or minor but it will represent opportunity depending upon how you handle it. In other words, in planning the individual call you should look forward to the unexpected and unanticipated in much the same ways you do in your gen-eral planning for the next several months ahead.

By that we mean that you know for certain that there will be a hurricane or a blizzard or good weather; the stock market will go up or down or just fluctuate; there will be political reper-cussions of some kind; there will be work stoppages or layoffs in some industries, full steam ahead in others. There may or may not be catastrophies of one kind or another, such as crashes, explosions, floods. If you knew in advance about any of these things and how they would affect your situation in deliveries, risks, or credit policies, to name a minor few, you could clean up. However, although you can't know these things in advance, you can be richly rewarded by planning over the next several month period how you would conduct yourself *if* this situation occurred or *if* that problem or opportunity arose.

Planning for the single sale should follow much the same pat-tern, but the approach should be different. The ingenious sales-man becomes very adept at planning each individual sale on the "spur of the moment." But he plans *every* sale in advance, even if it's only a few minutes in advance. The best way to do that is with a check list:

1. What is the objective of the call? To get an order, more counter space, a store promotion, an interview with the top brass? Of course, the end result is always an order, more business, better cooperation. But your pro-cedure will vary, depending upon exactly what you are going after on this particular call. In this case, you are going after a retail order—a promotion—the works. We will carry through this whole analysis on this basis.
2. You next will see the department supervisor or retail clerk for permission to take the inventory. You will want to rearrange the display in your favor. Don't ask,

"May I rearrange the display?" And don't rearrange without permission, even though you probably can't get it by asking direct. Rather plan in advance a way to put the clerk or supervisor in a good light by re-arrangement, or to keep them out of trouble with the boss. For example, you say, "I'll give you a tip that boosted Nellie Bly's sales down at Wilson's 50 per cent last month. It's quite simple; all she did was. . . . If you want, I'll get you started simply by a couple of minor revisions in the display." Now, have an alternative in the event of the unexpected—or of a negative response. "Actually, Mr. Jones has been very disappointed in his sales not increasing as fast as your next door competitor's and I should have put this plan in effect last time I was here. Should we go up and see Mr. Jones together?" Chances are you'll get permission.

3. Get the clerk to help you at the counter and you can engage in a little clerk training. This is a subject in itself, but the name of the game is to get your products exposed to the consumer. Regardless of what the clerk says about them, three-fourths of the battle is won just by getting consumer attention. The clerk says, "May I help you?" The consumer says, "I'm just looking, thank you." The clerk then says "Our X-4-3 products (your line) from $1.00 to $10.00 are shown over here." If the consumer shows any interest, the clerk either begins to show the merchandise or says, "Would you like to see (most popular model)" as she reaches for the product.

4. With the store inventory in hand, plan the recommended order which is to be presented to the buyer. As you prepare the recommended order, catalogue in your mind a *reason* for each item—in the event you are challenged. This will also help you prepare for the unexpected. You have already made your appointment with the buyer so you are now ready for the next broad category of the selling procedure.

How to Introduce the Sale

Keep in mind that the moment you face the buyer the sale has started and agreement is the keynote. You will recall that in Chapter 7 we discussed these areas of selling agreement. If you don't have them well in mind, you should review them again, as it will aid in the digest of the present material. In introducing the sale, two things are important:

1. You must set the mood or tenor for the sale and here's where most salesmen make a judgment mistake. They believe the buyer must be in a good frame of mind— he must be happy or cheerful or pleasant to make the sale come off. Not so. And there's little point in spending precious time in making an effort to put the buyer in a cheerful mood.

    You want the buyer to be in a receptive mood and your opening conversation should lead to that milepost. Don't open with, "How's business?" Or the weather, or the stockmarket, or the family. Tell him that it's sure nice to see him again—that he's looking well. And smile. Tell him you've got some good news—"And we all could use a little of that these days. Don't you agree?" He won't say no.

    Be ready for the unexpected—if he has a broken leg, he's been explaining it to every salesman for the past two weeks—but you can't ignore it. Get agreement that it's a shame these things have to happen but that time marches on. Expect him to be busy and thinking of other things to do besides talking to you. If the situation is different than that, it's all to your advantage. In any event, your selling pitch has begun and your first target is the buyer's receptiveness.

2. The second phase of introduction to the sale is to set the objective of your call. Here, too, you are asking for agreement, and it is well to be specific. You don't say, "Charlie, I'm here to sell you the biggest order you ever placed with me," or other words to that effect. Don't

apologize for not being there sooner—always imply that things are hot with you and time is elusive. It's true, anyway.

Do intimate that you have gone a little out of your way so that you could be of help to him with the hot promotion you have—but certainly don't overdo it. He won't believe you climbed over broken glass on your hands and knees—it would only weaken your story. Allow a minute or two for the pleasantries and to establish receptiveness, then say, "Charlie, I would normally be another week or two in getting in here but because what I have for you and a few of my other good customers is so strong I decided to high spot. The purpose of my visit is to set up an early fall promotion with advertising, window and counter tie-up, based upon two great specials we will have for that period. I am prepared to wrap the whole package up on this visit, even to the extent of settling on the stock you will need to make it come off successfully. Now—this all sounds like a big assignment but it's really quite simple and won't take much time if we get right on it. Ready to get started?"

Expect the unexpected, such as an interruption before you hardly get underway, but don't let it throw you. Keep foremost that you *must* first set an objective that is quite specific and then get agreement from the buyer that he is ready and willing to move on toward the objective. Don't deal in generalities or say that you are there to show the greatest new product innovation since the wheel or the hottest promotion in the industry.

Now that you have "sold" the buyer to be receptive and have settled with the buyer on your objective, you are into the sale.

How to Make the Selling Presentation

The average salesman believes that a selling presentation consists of offering the buyer a series of reasons to buy. Proceeding on this course only leads to a series of objections from the buyer. Then, too, it leaves no provision for the unexpected. Instead, this phase of selling should be viewed as a chance to present a few undisputable facts with the buyer's interests foremost.

Your facts must be in logical order leading to a successful conclusion. They must be understandable and understood. They must be directed toward the buyer's personal interests as well as his business interests. And finally, the facts should be presented on a conversational level so that the skills of perception can come into play to help provide direction.

> Charlie, because my company is a leader in its field it's their responsibility to come up with the best products and merchandising ideas in the industry—backed up with strong advertising. It's our job, yours and mine, to make these things work for you. Right?
>
> Well, a recent survey (show portfolio) shows there is a 7 per cent increase per year being spent for merchandise of this general class. There are more people shopping for these lines with more money to spend. With your stature in this market you really should be getting a bigger share. Agree?
>
> My company has decided to put their money where their mouth is and shoot the works. Here's the advertising that will reach your market—your customers (show portfolio). We are willing to spend this kind of money because we know you'll get the extra business to support it. Charlie, I think you can get increases that will make top people in both your company and mine sit up and take notice. At least we ought to try—o.k.?
>
> Now, here's how we do it (explain the offer—displays—promotion. Get the buyer to ask questions so that you are certain he understands). Now we can proceed in either of two ways. (*Note:* Give the buyer a choice between something and something—not something and nothing.) Which way do you think we ought to go, Charlie?

With this kind of a presentation, you are ready to close. Further, you have general agreement of the offer, you have the inventory and recommended order so that now all you have to settle are the details. Before we get to that, consider the unexpected in the selling present

1. The buyer disputes your facts—not lil *evidence* and he does not.

2. The buyer gets traumatic news over the telep.. in person. You stay calm, remember exactly where you were and what was covered. If it doesn't appear too serious, offer your help. If it does appear serious, offer to leave and take the matter up with someone else if he wishes. Often under these circumstances, you can write your own ticket—and you are expected to take this responsibility. Just say, "Look, you have other things to think about right now. Why don't you just let me go ahead and set up this promotion and handle all the details for you? I'll be completely responsible and I'll leave a copy of the order and a note on procedure."

3. The buyer is interrupted in such a way that it is evident he simply wants to break off the interview. In this instance, the buyer needs a shock treatment. "Mr. Buyer, we could be talking about the difference between profit and loss for your department for a whole year—just based on your success with this one offer."

Again, plan for the unexpected in the selling presentation phase—and plan to turn the unexpected to an advantage in completing the successful sale. Now for the close.

How to Get the Order

Asking for the order is really the most natural, simplest effort in the whole selling procedure. The reason—you have been asking for the order from the moment you walked into the store:

1. You anticipated the order by taking the stock inventory and pencilling in a suggested order.

2. You engaged in sales training with the clerk in anticipation of the order.

3. You rearranged the counter display and indicated where new displays should go in anticipation of the order.

4. As you sit with the buyer, with the inventory and suggested order in full view, you imply that he will buy.
5. You mention to the buyer that you have put the counter in shape and keyed the clerk up to do a better job—in anticipation of more stock.
6. You have set an objective that will call for back-up merchandise.
7. You have offered the buyer an alternative way to run the promotion—both ways will require that he buy.

There are three sure-fire steps to the successful close from this point:

1. Summarize briefly. Here are itemized the things discussed and the objectives of the interview.
2. Make a recommendation. This is the end result of the purpose of the interview.
3. Ask a question that provides the impetus for writing the order.

For example, after you have summarized and settled upon the displays, promotion, and advertising, you simply say, "Let's look at your current inventory and my suggestions for merchandise models you will need. Let me ask you—

a. How do you want the shipment to come out—50/50 the warehouse and the store or more directly to the counter?
b. I'd recommend a heavier inventory on Product A in ratio to Product B. What do you think?

These are known as double positives—any answer is a "yes" answer. You should take time right now to think of four or five double positives for your line to cinch agreement by the buyer on the order. It is by far the easiest, most direct technique. No matter what the buyer says, he is agreeing to buy.

The big problem in getting the order is getting the right order and getting the order large enough. Most buyers underbuy and most salesmen undersell. The tragedy is that no promotion can work with inadequate stock because:

1. The salesman, by underselling, indicates to the buyer he has doubts about the offer.
2. The buyer doesn't believe—and if he doesn't believe, it will not work.
3. The clerk doesn't try because she sees inadequate stock as the store's lack of confidence.
4. The consumer who doesn't see plenty of stock in evidence is not attracted to the offer.

"Buying right" are words that should be substituted for "closing the sale." In most cases, the salesman is so intent on getting the order that he settles on an inadequate order to reach the objective both he and the buyer have agreed upon. The buyer is inclined to "buy short" on the theory that he can always get the merchandise later (although he never does) and he will try to "buy short" if the salesman lets him.

Some salesmen, counting on buyer apathy, recommend a larger order than they think the customer will buy. This is all wrong. It is the salesman's responsibility as an expert to convince the buyer to buy right. If the salesman gives up, the buyer loses confidence, particularly after the promotion concept has already been proved right and the buyer has agreed to it. The salesman can only get and retain buyer confidence with complete integrity. His inventories must be honest and his selling statements accurate. He should make certain the buyer understands exactly what he is getting in terms of merchandise, terms, discounts, and delivery.

Stick to your recommended order. Tell the buyer that:

1. You spent time and thought on this order. You know what your customers are selling and the correct ratios. You are the expert.
2. You have figures to support the fact that consumers won't buy adequately from half empty displays in your line.
3. If he supports your promotion in all phases, i.e., advertising, in store display, clerk support, etc., your company will see that he doesn't get hurt, and will:

   a. Provide for an inventory adjustment exchange.

   b. Include him on a stock reducing program.

   c. Agree to transferring stock within your territory (look out for legal or tax complications).

Note: If your company doesn't have exchange and return policies, take this point up with your supervisor. No company should protect a retailer who does not give full support to its line. No company should protect either a timid buyer or a weak salesman. On the other hand, when an extraordinary commitment is made in good faith, it represents both retailer cooperation and strong salesmanship and this should not be penalized. Ingenious selling invites the extraordinary result.

4. Translate the order into terms of individual sales of each piece of merchandise. Put in his mind's eye a picture of people coming up to the counter as a result of the advertising, promotion and offer, and making purchases because of an adequate and inviting selection. Picture for him the enthusiasm his clerks will put forth with a good inventory to work from.

Now for the unexpected—suppose the buyer has agreed with your objective, likes your promotion and offer, has seemingly gone along in every respect, but balks at giving you a supporting size order. In this event, his reasons are probably these:

   a. He knows your competitor will come along with a good offer and he wants to support him too.

   b. He fears being tied so deeply (dependently) to one line.

The moment he says, "Let's cut Item A from 12 to 6 and Item B from 18 to 9," you have to ask, "Why?" His first answer will be, "Because it looks like too much." You reply, "Why do you think so?" When you took the inventory and wrote out the recommended quantity, you did it with a reason. You continue, "Last month without any effort you sold 7 of Item A and 11 of Item B. These quantities will only give you a few extra pieces to support your extra promotional efforts. You can't even afford to go after the business if you don't have the stock to sell. My recommendations are on the conservative side if anything."

If the buyer says, "I've got to support two lines in this department," your answer is "Charlie, I go along with that but we're talking about degree. Your customers are buying my line —that's where the dollar sales are coming from, and the dollar profits, too."

If the buyer is adamant, it is generally right to accept his decision in good grace. Rarely does ill feeling pay off. However, leave the matter with this remark, "You'll never know what you could do unless you have the stock to do it—and I do think you have a chance to be a hero with this proposition. My recommendation is still to go—you tell me."

In social as well as business contacts, persistence is frowned upon; your buyers don't like it and you won't win any popularity contests by employing it. But in selling, persistence pays off—use it.

Here's an exercise which will pay off: Using your product line, list as many objections as you can imagine that the buyer will use against the order size. Remember, in this exercise, he is going to buy—these objections refer to the quantities only. Now, come up with answers. The answers are important because they involve the whole presentation actually. They concern *turnover* on your line by the retailer in question and by his competitors. They involve dollar profits, good consumer selection, and many, many more things. Let's look at a few examples.

(1) *Buyer:* I've got six each of Products A and B so I can get by with only two of Product C.
Answer: You recognize you need Product C or you wouldn't order any. If you aren't going to order a selection, you simply won't make sales.

(2) *Buyer:* Your factory can supply me fast if I need more.
Answer: Right, but fast is three weeks at best before goods can be shipped, marked and at the counter. You've only ordered 12 and your reorder point is 6. You'll lose sales for three weeks with six or less pieces on display. You should order 24 and reorder at 12.

(3) *Buyer:* I can't give you all my open-to-buy.
Answer: The name of the game is greater dollar sales and profits. That's what open-to-buy is for. Your turnover will

give you open-to-buy for other products shortly—right now you need stock badly and you need the quantities I've indicated.

(4) *Buyer:* Cut those quantities in half and we can talk business. *Answer:* Please understand, Mr. Doe, that my recommendation is 100 per cent honest. I didn't make it hoping I could walk away with 50 per cent. To make this proposition pay off, you need these quantities—no more, no less.

Okay—it's your turn to raise your own buyer objections and your proposed answers. Write them down and review them. Remember, no objections on price, quality or merchandising elements. These have all been settled—the order in general is agreed. List only those objections on quantity or the *right* order, the order the buyer should buy.

The ingenious salesman will get the order; getting the right order will determine the extent of ingenious selling abilities. Now, let's move on to the final phase of the sales pattern.

How to Follow Up on the Sale

Most selling texts will advise you to make certain the buyer understands the terms of sale, the delivery conditions and other details of this nature. Good advice. You wouldn't want your diligent efforts to fall apart because of a misunderstood detail. But that's not exactly what we have in mind here in discussing follow-up.

You have completed a successful sale—you have sold the buyer the right order for him. You believe that, and he believes it too. But he still has to prove it. As it has been said, the proof of the pudding is in the eating. You had better give him all the help you can before you leave to make your proposition come off. The best formula for the order follow-up is to look for the problem areas. Let's explain that.

Example

Suppose you represent a line of small leather goods—travel kits, wallets, leather novelties. You have sold a large order for

fall and Christmas to be backed by retailer advertising and point
of sale promotion.

What has gone sour in the past on promotions of this kind?
What could have been done to have made these sour promotions
successful? How does the past experience apply to the present
situation?

Assume, for example, that the sour promotion was caused
because a full page newspaper advertisement ran on the day
of the biggest blizzard in the history of the state. How could
it have been saved?

1. The rest of the week the retailer could have pasted tear sheets
   of the advertisement in his window along with a big sign,
   "Blizzard Specials—This Week Only." A few of the items
   could be featured at special prices.
2. A special drawing with leather goods as prizes could be
   featured in the window along with the advertisement.
3. A special employee's discount could be announced.

Lesson 1—even an unavoidable circumstance can be rectified
if the retailer is prepared to do the necessary. Ingenious selling
prepares him.

Now, a previous promotion of this nature may have failed
because the clerks were not keyed in. They should be brought
in on the whole plan. Not only are they flattered by the recognition but the program won't succeed without it. Displays don't
get up and/or stay up. Merchandise is not featured. Oftentimes,
a sales clerk will deliberately run a promotion down because
she doesn't believe in it.

Following the sale decision, the people who will face the consumer should be appraised of details and their part in them.

1. They should be told what merchandise is coming and
   when it will arrive so that they can find a place for it.
2. They should be shown the displays involved, how to
   set them up and where they should be placed.
3. They should be advised of the advertising so that they
   can show a tear sheet at the counter and direct their
   efforts as a tie-in with the ad.

4. They should be treated as an important part of the team to make the whole promotion come off. There should be a period in your conversations with them for questions and answers.

Lesson 2—everybody who will take part in a retail promotion, window display people, advertising department people, retail clerks, even floor walkers, should be keyed in to the promotion and advised their function in it. Ingenious selling follow-up.

One salesman, upon completing promotion arrangements, would go to a nearby florist and obtain a couple of tasteful but inexpensive corsages to be delivered to the two salesgirls on the morning of the promotion effort. He would send a little card with each—"Bet you can have a $500 day today! Bill."—"Surprise yourself by beating last year's record! Bill."

Customers and friends ask the girls, "What's the occasion?" Anyway, how can the girl forget what to do when she's wearing your flowers all day to sweetly remind her?

Example

Suppose you represent a manufacturer of industrial oils for use with special milling machines. You have gone through a lot of tests and finally closed the sale.

It would be only natural to acquaint the factory people, engineers, and machine operators who will be using your product with its special features and advantages. If possible, you would want to show them firsthand how they could turn out better work easier.

In this case, your reorder won't come from the buyer but really from the machine operator, whose attitude is probably, "They're always telling me what to do and never asking my advice. Well, I'll tell them this new oil doesn't work." With good follow-up this won't happen.

Example

The salesman who sells mechanical products directly to the consumer, e.g., washing machines, dryers, even automobiles, has a follow-up problem he often overlooks. He doesn't insure himself against the customer who doesn't know how to "work" the product. After the sale is closed, he often just hands the customer an instruction book and sends him on his way without careful instructions. He assumes the customer knows what to do. Too often, if something goes wrong, the salesman becomes involved, which takes time and effort and costs the salesman a loss of earnings.

Regardless of what you are selling, or to whom, it pays to follow-up after the sale is closed—not only to cover the details and effect a thorough understanding but to insure that the sale will prove, in fact, satisfactory in every respect to the buyer as well as to you. This is a definite factor in ingenious selling. You will find that a majority of your satisfied customers will find a way to pay you again for the sale you follow-up properly.

Remember, to follow-up properly, look for the problem areas.

Let us now review this chapter briefly as an ingenious approach to the five important phases of the complete selling function—overcoming the unexpected:

1. *Approaching the Selling Situation.* This involves planning in advance for the individual call and all the activities prior to facing the buyer.
2. *Introduction to the Sale.* This requires putting the buyer in a receptive mood and getting agreement on your objective.
3. *Making the Selling Presentation.* This involves the proof that the objective is desirable for the buyer.
4. *Getting the Order.* By this time, the order is generally agreed. It requires skill in settling on the *right* quantities—displays, offers, and so on.
5. *Follow-up of the Sale.* No sale is complete until the buyer feels satisfaction with his purchase. The salesman can't wait for it but he can insure it.

Preparation for the sale and the proper conduct of it anticipates and employs the unexpected to assure a successful result.

11

Seventeen New and Different Approaches to Solving Seventeen Common Sales Problems More Effectively

As you have been studying this book and, at the same time, working your territory and cautiously applying some of the ingenious techniques you have acquired, you have also been learning a great deal more about yourself and your customer relationships. Think! Translate your thoughts to ideas, plans, techniques! Apply the ideas, plans and techniques to your selling processes! Reap the rewards!

Many salesmen simply do not think. A successful salesman does not require a high I.Q., nor really is this an essential in any profession. Average intelligence is enough for outstanding performance if it is properly used. Probably not one person in ten thousand is truly creative. It may even be next to impossible to *learn* to be creative. Any salesman with average intelligence can, however, learn to be ingenious just by using his thinking processes to full capacity.

A *Wall Street Journal* article of 27 September 1966 describes an effort by salesmen and men in other professions to improve their performances through the application of hypnosis. Success was reported by some. This should not be surprising to already successful salesmen. They know that a salesman can do almost anything he sets out to do if he believes in it implicitly and if he thinks it through deeply and then tells himself often enough that it really can be accomplished. Possibly this simple process is, in reality, a form of hypnosis.

Getting ideas and discovering new methods stems, as we have said before, from problem solving. You may refresh your memory by rereading Chapter 3. You will recall we used an example of an observation that was translated by a question into a sales problem. The sales problem required an answer. The answer required ideas. The ideas developed new business.

So we shall devote this chapter to sales problems, some of them new sales problems and others not so new. We will find answers through ideas gained in analyzing the problem. Then we will literally turn the problem into opportunity by ingenious use of the ideas. All of this is not quite as involved as it seems. Let's start with a broad subject, "How to size up the buyer," or, "How to handle a buyer once you've sized him up."

Now the problem is "Angry or grudge buyers," "Women buyers," "Inscrutable, silent, or talkative buyers," "Unsuccessful and successful buyers," "Chain store buyers," "Mom & Pop store buyers," "New buyers," "Old friend buyers," or you name them. They are all different and the problem cannot be reduced to a common denominator. Well—maybe not one, but a few? Yes —the solution to the problem of handling the "problem buyer" can be reduced to a few common denominators and there is an ingenious technique in arriving at them.

A. *The Number One Problem—Analyzing the Buyer*

Instead of "sizing up the buyer," think first of "sizing up the buying situation." Of primary consideration in this connection is that it must be determined who really makes the buying decision. Is it really the buyer? With a wholesaler, for example, it is often the sales manager. The buyer will not make the decision to buy a certain product or brand unless the sales manager indicates that he wants or needs it or can sell it. The buyer's responsibility is to determine colors, sizes, models, and quantities of each. He must keep track of the inventory, know shipping specifications, storage problems, delivery requirements in and out. He keeps the ball rolling once it is started—but he doesn't start it rolling. The sales manager does that.

It is quite obvious that the salesman doesn't "sell" the buyer. He "sells" the sales manager. And how does he do that? He sends in "turnover" orders. He holds sales meetings with the wholesaler's salesmen. He works with the wholesaler's salesmen. In other words, he "demonstrates" how the selling job for his products is accomplished with the retailer. He then convinces the sales manager (and other management) that there is great opportunity with his products or brands. After that, the counsel with the buyer and the writing of the order become somewhat routine. Make no mistake about it, however; the buyer is extremely important in this situation, although he does not make the initial buying decision.

Who do you deal with in your selling capacity? Who makes the essential buying decision? Does this person make only the initial decision or is he involved with all of the subsequent decisions too? This is necessary knowledge for two reasons:

a. In order to get your line in initially, you must talk to the right man—the decision maker. At this point you have nothing to lose—you can go right to the top.

b. After you have attained the initial decision, you must be careful of the "buyer's prerogatives." He is there for a purpose, and only on a rare occasion will you attempt to "go over his head."

With the life insurance salesman, the wife might really be the decision maker. But the husband pays the bills, agrees to the details and signs the contract.

Teenagers in the family often decide on the automobile by encouraging Dad not to be a "square." Their influence should not be overlooked.

The industrial salesman might have to sell engineers, production people, even the janitor! His business, of course, is with the purchasing department.

The consumer goods salesman, selling at the retail store level, may have to make a series of sales, sometimes starting with the retail clerk at the counter and going from there, through the buyer, to the merchandise manager or even the owner of the store. Once, however, the offer or promotion or line is accepted, the buyer is all important.

But remember in many, many situations, the buyer makes the initial decisions and all others that follow. In many other situations, the buyer is the only contact, regardless of the fact that others in the organization influence the buying decision. So what are the guide lines in sizing up the buying situation?

a. Ask questions. Ask other salesmen. Unless the salesman is a direct competitor, you can get good reliable information. Ask clerks, secretaries, department managers. Do not ask stockroom people, floor walkers, and others who have little connection. Be very diplomatic—and not too obvious. Identify yourself immediately: "My name is Tom Baker and I'm with the Sealtex Company." Let the clerk identify herself. "I'm here to discuss putting our brand into the store and I've always found the place to start is where the merchandise is sold. I wonder if you can give me a little information." Don't say, "Who's the boss?" or, "Who runs things around here?" Do say, "Who would you suggest I see first?" and, "What is the usual procedure?"

b. Practice awareness (Chapter 3). Check the local newspaper for the store's advertising. Look the store over— window displays, counter displays. What is the neighborhood atmosphere? Up and coming? Run down? What is the condition of your competitor's line in the store? If everything is shipshape, your attitude and presentation will reflect your respect for the people who are running a taut ship. If things are a bit shoddy, your attitude and presentation will reflect your willingness to be helpful in corrective measures.

c. Start with the purpose of getting to the right people quickly—without having to make the same presentation twice or even three times. The first selling job could well be selling the buyer on getting together with the merchandise manager for your presentation. Your attitude should be cordial, but businesslike and meaningful. Of course, if there is no alternative to your making two presentations, by all means make them. It won't hurt the buyer to hear your pitch twice—particularly if he will make all of the follow-up buying decisions.

Take an ingenious approach to sizing up the buying situation. It is as important to know where to go for the order and how to get there as it is to know how to control the actual presentation interview itself. You can save yourself hours of labor and many dollars in lost business by the correct accomplishment of this vital selling function.

B. *Problems Number Two through Fifteen—* *Fourteen "Type" Buyers*

Now that the buying situation has been determined, some tips on the ingenious handling of problem buyers is in order. Use of the word "buyer" in this connection might mean anyone to whom a presentation is made and a buying decision is expected. The easiest way to approach this subject is to individually analyze each problem area.

The (1) Upset, (2) Angry, or (3) Grudge Buyer

Most salesmen give up when they encounter a buyer of this category, and it is just luck if the situation turns out even remotely favorable. Yet there are many buyers with a low boiling point, and these are also just the types who carry a grudge because of past real or imagined insults. You can spot the buyer with a "chip on his shoulder" and plan your tactics accordingly. When something you say or do touches him off, that is when your ingenious selling training comes to the fore.

First, encourage him to get his problem "off his chest." The more he talks it out the less important it becomes to him. At this point you agree with him—not with his point but rather the seriousness of the problem and his right to be angry and upset.

Next, you appeal to his reason. The ingenious approach is to get over the point—diplomatically—that he is letting his attitude affect adversely his own and his company's best interests. It is only foolish for a buyer to let something result in a decision that can only hurt him. "Mr. Wilson, you have every right to be upset and I'm glad you brought the matter up because I can do something about it. I guess situations like this can all be solved in one way or another and after all, you wouldn't want something like this to affect your best interests."

Finally, you take advantage of the reaction which generally follows anger—this is a reaction akin to embarrassment or "face saving." You help it along as much as possible by overlooking the episode and proceeding with your selling conversation. Your perception will tell you that the buyer is more attentive and cautiously more cooperative. Indeed, it often turns out that the incident is more of an advantage than a handicap.

(4) The Woman Buyer

It is a twist of nature that women are homemakers and men are breadwinners. In many respects, characteristics would indicate that things should be the other way around. Generally, women in business have more patience, more perception, are more diligent and dependable and are more dedicated, than are their counterparts. In matters of taste and style they are usually more adept than men—and in matters of tact and diplomacy, too. Of course, this is opinion—you can take it or leave it.

On the other hand, women make emotional decisions—they take things personally. An argument is not just a debate, but rather a series of sentences that mean that the arguer doesn't like her. So, she won't like him or agree with him in any way. Too often, to her a sales conversation is an argument. But, fortunately, women must feel needed and, because of that fact, *you* don't have to make *your* sales interviews arguments. Of course, this is opinion also—but what other choice do you have?

Seriously, the ingenious way to slant your sales conversation to the woman buyer is to show how your proposition will help her fulfill her obligation as a needed and necessary employee. You must convince her that by accepting your offer she is but completing her role. And the offer had better live up to what you claim of it or she will perceive it. Obviously, however, it will live up to expectations if she believes in it because she will make it work—you see, that's a part of her role, too.

A few rules: (a) Don't argue. If she takes exception, admit that her reasons are sound, but that she might look at it this way. . . . (b) Do use emotional appeals. Picture the customers being handled pleasantly but profitably at the counters. (c) Don't be overly friendly. Be helpful. Try to be remembered as a "nice man."

One last word. There will be more and more women buyers because they are good at it, and because, in many respects, it is a detailed job. You don't have to be a psychologist to sell women successfully but you will have to plan more diligently and execute your plan differently than with the male of the species.

(5) *Inscrutable and* (6) *Silent Buyers*

The problem here is getting a reaction. You do all the talking and never know how well you are doing until you reach the end of your presentation and the buyer says, "Try me next time." You can't allow this to happen because there is no returning to the point where you lost the buyer's interest and attention.

Ask strong questions. By that we don't mean just attempting to get a response by asking for agreement. This calls for a minor revision in your presentation. Instead of questions, such as, "How does this fit in with your thinking?" or, "Don't you agree?" (where an "O.K." or "Yes" will suffice for an answer), your conversation will call for questions that require a more comprehensive reply.

Example

Mr. Wilson, this promotion calls for advertising under our cooperative advertising plan. Now your store uses television, radio and newspaper. I'd like to get your ideas on which you would choose for this line and why—what are you thinking?

Another example:

Mr. Williams, the way I see it, the time has come for a show-down on whether your department can attain a 20 per cent increase in sales and 25 per cent increase in profits similar to the Rogers and Owens figures I just showed to you. Please tell me what you see in the operation of this example department as differing from the operation of your own?

Warning—don't get the sales conversation on fishing, golf, vacations, the wife and kids, or anything other than business. You'll find your silent buyer suddenly turn talkative.

Incidentally, the (7) *Talkative Buyer* is handled in just the opposite manner from the Silent Buyer. Only agreement questions should be asked, or no questions at all. You will be able to perceive how the interview is going with the buyer's normal interruptions. The problem here will be staying on the subject without too many time-consuming diversions.

(8) *Successful and* (9) *Unsuccessful Buyers*

It doesn't take much perception on your part to determine which of your buyers are making a success of their efforts and which are not. Both types represent opportunity; each requires a slightly different technique.

Oddly enough, most unsuccessful buyers are those who "stand on their own." They have strong opinions, won't let salesmen help them much. They "know their business" and won't take much advice. They are very hard to sell the first time because they are committed to a policy which they do not want to admit is wrong.

Take what we term the "priest" approach. Confession is good for the soul. The tenor of your presentation should be that the world is rapidly changing and that we're in a rocket economy. You have found your most successful accounts taking a real hard look into their operations—and drastically changing them. For example, "In my line. . . ." Of course, all of your interviews incorporate a sense of urgency but in the case of the unsuccessful buyer it should be more pronounced.

The successful buyer can prove less of a problem even though he has been successful without your line. The reason—he is willing to exploit an opportunity if he recognizes it. Your offer spells opportunity and if you are prepared, and you execute your presentation properly, this is a breeze. As they say in the theatre, this is one "according to the script."

(10) Chain Store Buyers

We could get into the pros and cons of the "canned sales talk" at this juncture because of the time element involved in the chain store interview. The problem with the chain store buyer is twofold: (a) the buying or review committee (see Chapter 9), and (b) the time element. We shall deal here with the latter. In most large chains, so-called buying hours are set at fifteen minute intervals for two two-hour periods each day, 10:00 A.M. to 12 Noon and 2:00 P.M. to 4:00 P.M. These hours are without appointment, although it is best to make one even though you may have to wait. *These are the advantages:*

1. Although the order is decided upon at once, the actual order writing comes later and does not take up interview time.
2. The buyer is familiar with merchandising and marketing techniques and involved explanations are not necessary.
3. The interview is free of interruptions and the buyer is a trained interviewer who actually helps you get your presentation across.
4. The buyer is neutral and has no loyalties except to his company. He is trained to be objective and unemotional.

These are the disadvantages:

1. The door is shut when the time is up. The buyer will close off the interview without a decision—either yes or no.
2. The buyer will try to get all he can in discount, advertising, display, etc. He is taught to be suspicious that

he is not getting everything that someone else is getting. He will withhold a decision if he believes that next time you will offer more. This exists even though most of these things are governed by statute—and the buyer knows it.

3. The stakes are high and much preparation time is necessary and often additional call backs are necessary. A failure is costly.

4. Because of many branch stores, it is difficult to know what the chain is doing on your line compared to your competitors. You can't have an accurate counter display picture. Chain records and data are not available to you.

A careful review of advantages and disadvantages will give you clues to your approach to the chain store buyer. Read each one, think about it and make some notes pertinent to your merchandise line. After you have done that, outline a "canned" presentation for your chain buyers. We haven't discussed "canned" presentations and we won't, because all interviews are "canned." The only pros and cons about this subject is the matter of degree. Now rehearse.

Ten minutes of carefully prepared presentation, well executed at a moderate rate and without interruption, can be ample to get your program successfully sold. That leaves five minutes for order details and questions. Order writing, as we have said, comes later. Remember, a chain buyer will make a $25,000 investment decision more easily than a smaller buyer will make a $1,000 decision. In both cases—be prepared.

(*11*) *The Small Store Buyer*

(*12*) *The "New" Buyer*

(*13*) *The "Old Friend" Buyer*

(*14*) *All Other "Problem" Buyers*

We hope the analysis of the ten buyer types rev
been helpful to you. Actually, however, the whole
tended to provide you with a technique to help y
the bottom of your own buyer problems. Let's c
few to help you get the picture more clearly.

What would you say are the problems with the small store
buyer? Well, for one thing, your business comes in dribs and
drabs and you can't afford much time—yet he has interruptions,
he is busy and cares little about your time. He knows that from
a distribution standpoint you need him. It just stands to reason
that the more of your merchandise that is exposed, the more
of it will sell.

Now you can list other problems with the small buyer, but
let's concentrate on the one outlined to illustrate procedure
purposes. The problem calls for an answer; the answer calls for
ideas. Here's one:

Suppose you have a brief outline of your offer attractively
typed with a display illustration but without prices or costs.
Upon arriving at the store you shake hands with the buyer,
hand him the outline and say, "This is the display and proposition I want you to consider on this trip. Why don't you look it
over while I get the inventory? I'll be right back." He can't
turn you down without knowing the price. He will have a few
questions. You make your briefed presentation to a more in-
formed audience.

Let's look at some others. What is the problem with the "new"
buyer? Principally, the problem is that you have learned how to
work with the "old" buyer—he's been trained, so to speak. Now
you have to start over, and that's a delicate situation. New buyers often want to sweep clean—question everything that's been
done before.

How to solve this problem? This one is up to you. Most
salesmen have it, so now, using the technique outlined, develop
your own ingenious solution.

How about the "old friend" buyer? This fellow has gotten so
close to you that he sells *you*. You've put yourself in a position

where he's hurting himself with your line because of your close personal association.

Here's a hint—better tell him outright about your problem and prepare in advance how you are going to do it. Notebook ready? Work out your own ingenious solution to this "problem buyer," too.

Now list others of your "problem buyers" and go through the outline techniques above.

1. Describe the problems.
2. Write down some ideas for solving each individually.
3. Practice application of the ideas.

If this preparation doesn't swell your order book, you're with the wrong company—it certainly can't be the fault of your effectiveness as a salesman.

C. Problem Number Fifteen—The "Too Big" Program

At this point, we will want to analyze some general problems common to most selling and employ some ingenious means to solve them.

Problem: My program is big and unwieldy. I just can't seem to get it all sold. My customers pick and choose. My interviews are so long that I'm conscious of trying to hurry and it affects my effectiveness in closing.

Well, that sounds like a mouthful but it is just one problem and a mighty costly one. The solution lies in a technique which we shall title "Umbrella Selling." By this, we first mean finding a common "Umbrella" that covers all the seeming loose ends of your products and merchandising offers and brings them together. Now, you present the "Umbrella" idea as the opener and fit in all the pieces as you go along. Example:

Suppose you are selling luggage and your line consists of six separate price ranges of men's luggage and four of women's. Each range has a number of pieces, i.e., club bag, one-suiter, two-suiter, wardrobe, etc. Each range also incorporates a different model and comes in several colors and materials.

It is now April and your company is taking orders for September College Back to School. National advertising will appear in magazines and on T.V. A dealer advertising and display plan will be in effect. Certain college styled, medium priced models will be featured. Now, go back and read the problem again. Done that? Let's look for the "Umbrella."

Assume your selling story surrounds itself around the fact that greater dollar sales and profits are possible for the retailer only by selling better quality, higher priced luggage. There is an abundance of low priced and cut priced selling in the industry, but the bottom of the market is bottom heavy. Yet you know that the college market is economy minded as well as style and quality minded.

So you decide your "Umbrella" will be *Economy*. The better construction and material of your luggage, the better all-round quality, will outlast 20 per cent cheaper luggage three to one. This is definite economy. The college bound student can own the handsome styles he wants and save money. An outline of your presentation goes something like this:

Mr. Retailer, for back to school this year, we are selling Economy with a capital E. No need for you to feature unprofitable lines without style or appeal on a price basis. Your whole effort—in your advertising, on your counter, with your clerk training, should be that the better quality of this line will provide far better service, satisfaction and economy. You will feature the college appealing models in this advertisement (go through it) and carry a good selection of all models in other prices so that you can sell quality both down and up. With well directed advertising, window and counter effort and adequate stock, this line can get you the lion's share of the back to school market in your area.

Note how the Umbrella "Economy" overcomes price objection before it arises, and allows the whole line to fit in. Note how well organized the presentation becomes with a central theme to hold it together.

Have you ever noticed how certain related things hang together: pens, pencils, writing paper, etc.? Men's shaving cream, hair dressings and aftershave are other obvious examples. Yet a consumer can be, and is, attracted to completely dissimilar products. The fact is that totally different products can be put side by side and sell well. The real reason that related products are displayed together is so that people can find them.

The lesson here for you is that you can group totally dissimilar products together and get them all presented so long as you have an "Umbrella." The "Umbrella" should be a *benefit*—to the consumer, the retailer, the wholesaler, the industrial accounts. A benefit, as you know, is not what the product or service is, but what satisfaction the user gets from it. A camper, for example, is not just a means of sleeping and eating away from home, but rather a wonderful vacation in the north woods. Who could sell color T.V. by describing how it works? The retailer and wholesaler want a plan for greater sales and profits. The industrial user wants cost economy.

So your "Umbrella" should be an all-encompassing benefit, a way to tie your program together for simpler organization and presentation.

D. Problem Number Sixteen—Too Much Selling Material

Problem: My company supplies me with a wealth of portfolios, catalogue selling sheets, brochures, special promotional pieces. Besides that, I have samples, visual aids, order books, record material and report forms. I am certain I could be more effective if I could get these things organized properly to find them the split second I need them.

Visual aids of all types, portfolios, selling sheets, photographs, testimonials, fact books (for company policy), and many other forms, are tremendously effective. Too few salesmen use them well or even at all because they are cumbersome and unwieldy. But the visual aid gives believability to the salesman's story because the company is backing him up in print. A picture is worth a thousand words—and that's the clue to organizing and using visuals.

First, you have to think of visuals as making your selling job easier, not harder. You have to think of them as shortening your selling time, not lengthening it. You have to think of visuals as keeping you better organized, not less. Once you've sold yourself, you've got it made. Here's how—first think of a certain customer and get a notebook ready.

a. Outline a planned presentation from the moment you greet the buyer until you close the order book and say goodbye. Outline, in as much detail as necessary, the points you would make in the order you would make them. Write down how you would ask for the order and the information you would need to write the order.

b. Now go over and check each portion of your presentation that would be strengthened with visual proof—a customer testimonial, a consumer or trade advertisement, a company policy (on price, for example), a photograph of a display. Make a list of the visuals (or verified facts) that would lend credence to your presentation.

c. Go through all of your company material and lift out those things that will visually support your presentation and get them in order. If there is information you do not have (such as sale rate of certain colors as compared to others, etc.), ask your supervisor to get it for you. Now put all your visuals in the order that you will use them. No matter if they are of different sizes and form—put them in order even if you carry them loose in a separate folder.

d. Now go through your outline and the visuals to see if they all fit. Memorize the salient points you want to make in the proper order. Now, with the visuals loose in front of you, rehearse the presentation using the visuals.

Most salesmen organize their material in their sample and carrying cases in such a way that they hope they can find it when they need it. Instead, they should organize how they will use the material and they will always have it available as they need it. You do it the latter way and your order book will reflect the difference.

E. Problem Number Seventeen—Price

There are many aspects of the problem of price; in fact, the problems of each company and each salesman within each company are different. A wholesaler cannot be told legally at what price he should resell a product. A few states have fair trade statutes governing consumer prices on certain registered lines. Brand names and products are closely imitated at lower prices. Private labels become new brand labels.

There is no point in repeating that ultimate users of all products or services are interested in value and not price. Overcoming price objections is not a difficult problem for any salesman providing one thing is true—the salesman must believe implicitly that his prices are fair and reasonable and that they represent real value. Any price problems can be resolved if this is true. Nothing less will suffice.

You should look first at yourself if you have a price problem. Study your products or services from a price and value standpoint. Consider such comparative aspects as long life, pride of ownership, wearability, desirability, and others. Compare prices in your industry. Now sell yourself and your price problems are over. Why?

Because you can turn this new belief into opportunity by bringing the subject up to the customer before he mentions it. You say, "One thing I want to mention as a real asset for you in our business is our price structure. . . ." While you are thinking up ways to justify your pricing policies, you are creating selling ammunition to use with your customer.

This whole chapter has been devoted to problem solving techniques. Each small aspect of the whole selling function should be looked upon as a problem to be overcome. Remember, problems demand solutions and solutions require ideas—this is where ideas come from. Ideas give rise to *ingenious selling.*

12

The Do's and Don't's for
Moving Ahead with
Your Company

This chapter will incorporate practical and ingenious measures to put you in a favorable light for advancement with your company. Most salesmen believe that if they do a creditable job they will be recognized and considered for promotion. This doesn't necessarily follow—in fact, it may rarely follow. Even an outstanding record, while it may be warmly recognized and appreciated, does not, even as a rule, carry with it much consideration for personal growth.

Yet, management people at every level are sorely needed. An issue of *Dun's Review* points out ". . . the most wanted man in industry today is the administrator, the man who is skilled in general management—not just chief executives, but executive vice presidents, regional and branch managers and executive assistants as well . . ." Everywhere is heard that the most pressing task of industry is the development of managers. Why, then, this paradox when it comes to salesmen? *Why do companies continually go outside for executive talent?* In the last ten years 46 new executive recruiting agencies have appeared in New York alone.

There are reasons. First, let's break down management people into two categories—the professionals and the administrators. To begin with, salesmen, accountants, lawyers, and engineers are professionals. As they assume more responsibilities that come with promotion they also assume more administrative duties; finally they reach an assignment level that is totally administrative. But let's look at salesmen exclusively.

First off, salesmen have very little opportunity to experience phases of the business other than marketing, merchandising and selling. It is a rare company that charges its sales force with profit accountability, and even when it does all that is involved with the salesman is a compensation plan—his job responsibilities remain strictly with selling. The salesman is too remote for real exposure with finance, research, production and other aspects of general management.

Next consideration—good salesmen are hard to come by. The company who has a profitable volume producer is naturally loath to change that situation. And the salesman in question can, by this time, be in an income bracket that makes a management step up actually an income step down. Often companies use a stop-gap supervisory promotional assignment for outstanding salesmen. This stop-gap is known as the district manager. The district manager has certain key accounts of his own, and may have other selling assignments, but his principal concern is supervising a few other salesmen. The competent district manager is invaluable in three ways: (1) as a producer, (2) as a supervisor, (3) as a candidate for greater management responsibilities.

All right now, let's stop right here and analyze what we have been talking about. We have said, in effect, that selling experience alone, even personal selling excellence, is not enough to recommend promotion. Management, to give a salesman exposure to other facets of the business, must take a great risk. The risk is that the salesman won't adapt himself well enough to an administrative type of assignment, or absorb business acumen in the areas required for management growth. In either case, then, they don't gain a manager and they lose a salesman. Misfits in management most often occur when a salesman is moved several steps up the ladder too quickly. A safer means from a management standpoint is to promote within sales a step at a time.

You should evaluate your company in this "growth opportunity" light. Is there a semisupervisory position just above yours, say as a district manager, that will permit you to attend manager training sessions, become more closely associated with other facets of the business and give you exposure to management "profit" thinking? If so, good. It gives you two distinct areas for growth—one, a certain (but slower) process to district manager, branch manager, regional manager, specialized manager (such as wholesale, syndicate, retail, etc.), and then to division or general sales manager. The other area for growth is still movement directly out of the sales force to another partly related or even a nonrelated assignment.

We are soon going to bring all of these things into their proper focus, but there is yet another element to examine before that can happen. We shall want to look at the completely unrealistic attitude with which many salesmen look upon management assignments. To do this, rather than list the salesman's ofttimes unrealistic view, let us evaluate some of the responsibilities and attributes required for top sales management.

Among other things, the sales manager is responsible for:

1. Forecasts. He must predict, in light of his merchandising programs, new products, economic conditions and budgets, what his sales force is going to sell, ship, bill and deliver—by product category. And he had better be optimistic or well prepared to explain why he is not! He had also better be accurate, because his budget depends upon it.
2. Budgets. He plans to deliver this forecasted business to his company at a sales cost that will make it profitable business. He must budget thousands of expenses.
3. Policies. He must see to it that the policies of his company are conducive to the easy flow of business procedure. He must translate all company policies into assets.
4. Territory structure. He must structure territories to get all the business possible based upon his company's position, and his salesmen's capabilities.

5. Compensation. He must plan a program that will provide incentive and a fair income for the people who report to him and will yet satisfy cost-conscious management.
6. Expenses and controls. He must provide a plan that will control expenses and maintain utmost efficiency for his entire field operation.
7. Volume and profit. Multitudes of sales decisions must be made with both of these factors equally considered. His decisions are conveyed in a deluge of correspondence, bulletins, personal conferences and meetings.
8. He must maintain discipline. Delegate responsibility and authority. Make fast and accurate "on the spot" decisions. Provide well trained and competent supervision.
9. He must be knowledgeable about training, recruitment, human values, and up-to-the-minute selling and marketing facts.
10. He must get along with his superiors and subordinates on a basis of mutual respect. He cannot afford indulgence with himself or the people who report to him either directly or indirectly.

All of this is a great challenge because, in addition, the sales manager must be a public speaker, meeting organizer, copywriter, trade relations director, and possess a host of other attributes not the least of which is a thorough and practical familiarity with salesmanship. And he must know the peculiar traits of his industry thoroughly.

It is only natural for the salesman to look on the sales manager's job as a sort of Mecca. What could the sales manager possibly do with all his time? Besides, consider the great security he has! This is what we refer to as unrealistic, but we most certainly don't want to imply that such a job is unattainable. Not at all. What we do want to caution against is reaching a job level you are not yet prepared for and failing it. And no matter what anyone tells you, you can't go back. So, by all means, take a realistic view of what you're striving for. If you do you'll be ready for it when you get it.

Today, field sales assignments are, in many cases, a career unto themselves. They incorporate good benefit programs for health, disability, and retirement. They provide for earnings and responsibilities advancements within the full sales areas. The same situation applies in other professions—even in medicine and in law. The salesman can and does often lock his total future into field selling successfully. Should he then *plan* for a total field sales career?

We advise against it. We advise against the attitude of "work hard, do what's told, stay on the right side of the boss, and you'll get ahead." We believe it *wise* to "hitch your wagon to a star." We feel that only by aspiring for higher goals can you attain any goal. Shoot for the top job but recognize that you have a self-development responsibility that goes hand in hand with your aspirations. By all means be realistic.

Do set a final goal for yourself that is realistically lofty—and with intermediate milepost goals along the way. Don't expect to attain each milepost without diligent and ingenious application of your experience and talent. Now you are off to a good start. So, let's examine the bits and pieces that will provide the "something extra" required for promotional growth.

Someone, or even several people, will enter into a decision to give you more responsibility, an additional assignment and more money. It is not only what you are that counts but also what others think you are. If several others are involved in making a growth decision for or against you, remember that each will see you a little differently. It is important to you that each has an image of you closely resembling the image you have of yourself. So, initially, you have a communications problem to be solved.

Communications with whom? First, not just your immediate supervisor. You will want to work closely with him, you need his respect and his support, but you must recognize he does not make an advancement decision concerning you. He often does have a veto power, however, and a decision might hang on whether he puts in a good word. It's your supervisor's job to know a lot about you and confirm or deny what others think of you.

Your communications problem really starts with the second level of sales management, such as the regional manager (your boss's boss) and then perhaps with two other levels above that. The idea is to get your name into the mill as "someone to watch"—and then keep it there. This can only be accomplished if handled very adroitly. The first prerequisite is doing an outstanding job in your present assignment. The second prerequisite is a plan:

Plan—Part One

Don't start too soon. Get your feet on the ground in the job you're presently assigned. It normally takes two years to get "comfortable" in an initial sales assignment. Your company gets to know you and what's more important, you get to know your company. Here are some things to be watchful about:

a. What is the attitude, as you interpret it, of top management toward the sales force? Do they attend sales meetings—and/or participate in them? Are they individually interested in the salesmen? Do they seem to welcome and accept ideas from the field? Do they try to understand field sales problems and attempt to find answers?

   You, of course, will have to weigh these attitudes in your own way as to whether they will affect your opportunities for growth and even your willingness to pursue your ambitions. To get a "fix" on management attitude you can obtain clues from correspondence, supervisor contacts, sales meetings, telephone conversations, bulletins, and even from the quality and fitness of your portfolios, brochures, point-of-sale material and other merchandising helps.

b. Are there a good percentage of management people who got their start in the field? Over a period of time, inquire into the background of middle level executives with your company. Remember, sales-oriented people understand and are more considerate of other sales people. Some management groups are suspicious of field sales people. They think of them as being "sharp." Unfortunately, in too many cases, these suspicions are not entirely unfounded. Honesty and straightforwardness are still great assets.

c. How do policies, programs, and marketing techniques measure up to your competitor's? Is your management alert to new trends in the industry? Don't assume there is opportunity for you in your company because "these people need help." Chances are good that if this situation existed management wouldn't recognize you as someone who could really help anyway. That is often the problem with companies in trouble. They look outside for problem-solvers. However, even if the going may be rough for your company, if your management is on the ball your promotion chances are good because troubles are temporary.

d. Even if your company goes outside for management help, don't be over-alarmed about your chances for advancement. This often happens to good companies who become lax about development programs for their own people. Remember the least desirable thing to do is to go outside. If insiders can qualify they will get first choice.

Plan—Part Two

During the period while you are "getting your feet on the ground," you can be establishing your lines of communications. Earn the respect of your immediate supervisor and always keep the lines of communication open with him. Reread "Working With Your Supervisor" in Chapter 9. Maintain your relationship on a business basis only.

Keep up to date in your retail correspondence, reports and follow-up assignments. Establish a reputation as trustworthy and steady with the credit and correspondence departments. Be dependable. If you are inclined to forget—make notes.

At sales meetings, meet people in management. Let them know who you are and don't leave it to chance. Even though you have met before say, "Mr. Burkholder, I'm John Calhoun from Atlanta. We've met before, but I just wanted to be re-membered to you." Have something else ready to say in the event your greeter doesn't introduce a subject.

On these occasions, don't make suggestions, or start a con-versation on a deep, controversial subject. Don't try to give yourself a "pat on the back" either. An interesting, timely busi-ness subject, with or without a territory reference, will put you in a better light than anything else.

Sales meetings are busy times for first and second level sales personnel. Nevertheless, try to get some casual time in with your second level manager. Let your supervisor know you are attempting to get better acquainted with the next higher level of management. If your relations are right with him, he won't stand in your way. However, prepare for this chance meeting carefully. Point up a current sales problem you are having in your territory and outline the plan you are using to solve it. However, always ask, "Do you have any suggestions?" Try to keep the conversation pleasant but concise. Leave the impres-sion that you are on top of your territory situation.

Plan—Part Three

We are still on the subject of your communications with top level people in your company concerning your personal growth. We have covered the initial introductory period of getting your feet on the ground in your job. You have now reached a point where the campaign begins for advancement. The most impor-tant thing you can reach for at this juncture is the chance to obtain a wider knowledge of your business and industry.

You will already have done the following:

a. Read a Standard and Poor's (or other) report on your com-pany and also on competitors' companies. Get the facts pretty well in mind on earnings and dividends over a period of time. Know the percentage of business done on certain product lines.

b. Read current stockholder reports on your own and com-petitors' companies. Study Profit and Loss and Balance sheets.

c. Kept up on the current business situation by regularly reading the financial pages of your newspaper. Interest yourself in occasional articles in the *Wall Street Journal, Forbes, Fortune* and other business magazines.

A great source of valuable knowledge to you is operational details of your *customers'* businesses. We have discussed the value of this kind of information in relation to your day-to-day selling activities. However, it can be even more valuable a couple of promotions later when you may be called upon to translate a company program in the light of a certain classification of trade. From an immediate standpoint, a remark made by your regional manager to the general sales manager such as, "You know, Harry has more knowledge of the drug business than anyone in my sales force," helps your stature immeasurably. It's important to your current sales effort that you have all of this general and specific business knowledge and it's just as important that because of it management people look upon you as a "comer."

You are now ready for a scheduled get-together meeting with your regional manager at your next sales meeting. This is not a haphazard meeting. You write to him a few days prior to the meeting, sending a copy to your supervisor. You acknowledge that meetings are hectic but that you just don't have a chance to see him at another time and you need a few uninterrupted minutes to discuss something of importance. If, at the meeting, you are thrown together at a cocktail party and he says, "Harry, what was that you wanted to see me about?" don't discuss it. Just say, "I'd rather have a few minutes under different circumstances—how about breakfast tomorrow morning?"

When you do get alone make it worth your while and his. Don't beat about the bush but use a direct approach.

As you may have suspected, the subject I want to discuss briefly is *me*. Eventually I want to hold an administrative management position with this company. I'm convinced, from what I read and experience, that the company has a bright future. I want to share in it and contribute to it and I know I can do that. I also know that while my field sales experience and "know how" is invaluable, I must have a wider knowledge in finance, personnel, research, and production. Possibly you can give me a bit of advice on how I can go about this. I do know that the district managers get some special management training and do get into headquarters for meetings. Possibly this is the area I should shoot for first. One thing—I do want you to know I'm not impatient. I like my job; I feel I'm making headway. On the other hand, I know the company is looking for young managers and I want to move as fast as my learning processes permit.

The presentation would obviously be more conversational than illustrated here, but these are the salient topics to be covered. You won't get immediate advice and don't expect it. You'll probably get:

Harry, let me give this subject some thought. I think you're already making progress and you haven't been with us long. Just go back and give it all you've got. Meanwhile, I'll talk to people back at headquarters and one of these days I'll have another chat with you.

You'll have to be satisfied with that.

The next time you see your supervisor be certain to tell him that, as planned, on the occasion of the last sales meeting you talked with the regional manager on the subject of advancement. Treat the subject candidly but seriously. Go back to work with diligence and forget your ambitions.

Now and then a solid suggestion to be directed to a product manager, branch manager or whoever, will occur to you. Make a note of it, give it careful thought and then write a letter to the management person most concerned with it. Be modest. Don't assume that this is something no one has ever thought of before. In this way, even if your suggestion has already been tried and rejected, you will still get credit for ingenious thinking. Don't shower management with suggestions. Make certain your suggestions are well thought through as to their practicality. Think from the standpoint of the company. For example, a labor saving suggestion for salesmen should not just relieve salesmen of a burden but must be of value to the company in greater efficiency and greater company return.

Plan—Part Four

If you have been applying good principles of self-development to your selling efforts and practicing the arts and skills of ingenious selling, you can be certain that you are being watched. You may not get a direct response to your regional manager interview for six months or so but you will perceive from management's attitude that you are not going unnoticed. If you are aware that this is the case you can afford to be patient. But in six months or so, you are entitled to a positive response from your regional manager interview which can be either (1) We've got you definitely in mind when the opportunity presents itself, or (2) We think you have growth potential but be patient. You need more sales experience.

With either of these answers you might now ask about some extracurricular management courses being given in your area that might be of help and interest to you. American Management Association and other organizations hold several day sessions on various aspects of management problems. Your company knows of these sessions and perhaps could make one or two available to you. At the same time, colleges and universities have practical nighttime courses that might be worth investigating. Your company record shows your experience and schooling. Make certain that any special training you have is made known and is put on your record.

While we are on this subject of schooling, let's point out that there has been no mention of *prerequisites* for growth and management assignments. There are two reasons for this omission:

1. Enlightened management recognizes that, in promoting from within, it has the opportunity of making decisions based upon actual values and not assumed ones. Now this does not imply that a college degree is not a factor nor that special training is not helpful. How-

ever, once the initial sales position is assigned, a decision has largely been reached regarding the merit of
the college degree. And, the company and/or the employee can always provide the special training that may
be required above experience.

2. The same goes for those special qualities necessary for
a successful management career. The quality of getting
along with people and of earning their respect, of good
personal organization, of logical decision making, and
all the others, were actually prerequisites for getting
the sales job in the first place. Success in the sales assignment attests to the further development of these
qualities.

We have devoted a whole book to exploiting the talents and
skills necessary to successful pursuit of present and future tasks.
There is no purpose in delineating them all again.

So, on to the final follow-up of our campaign for recognition
and advancement. We have to assume that you like and respect
the company who employs you or you wouldn't be attempting
advancement with them. If this does not hold in your current
position, it will not hold in the next or the one following either.
Therefore, we must now consider that the company may decide
(1) that they want to wait two to five more years and take the
chance of losing you within that time, or (2) that you have
growth and earnings increase possibilities within your present
assignment and that is as far as they intend to go.

If your company arrives at either of these decisions, they will
only tell you that a promotion is not possible at this time and
that they will review it again in another year. However, at the
conclusion of a three year or so period, you are entitled to an
answer, either a positive one or one of postponement. Then, of
course, it becomes a decision making period for you. One quali-
fication—if this is your first sales assignment and/or if you are
under thirty, you must allow yourself and your company more
time for maturity. Whether true or not, your company believes

that business acumen comes with maturity—and you won't change that. Now . . .

Write a letter to the general sales manager or whoever is the top man closest to your field sales assignment requesting an audience. Before you mail, show and discuss it with your supervisor and make a copy for your Regional Manager. Point out that you have respect for the company's aims and principles, and for its management. From your vantage point you have great confidence in its future growth possibilities. Explain that you feel that you can contribute more to that growth in an upward assignment and specifically name the assignment and field it is in, if at all possible. Examples: Product Manager or Sales Promotion Manager (ingenious selling experience lends itself to creative market planning and creative merchandise programming), District Sales Manager (combines selling and sales supervision with some administration), Business Research Manager (may require some special training which the company can provide), Sales Training Director (combines ingenious selling experience with teaching qualities), Sales Administration Manager (territory structuring, compensation programs, carrying equipment, field communications). These are but a few of the opportunities which can be afforded directly from field sales.

Don't let your letter imply urgency—use the words "considered for." At the same time, don't use the word "satisfied" in any mention of your present position. It is assumed you are satisfied with your relationship with the company and your progress or you wouldn't be inquiring about your possibilities for promotion. Do be explicit that you want the opportunity of getting broader knowledge of company operation which the described promotion will give you.

This is not a letter of application. You do not state your qualifications except in a broad way, or if you have specialized training that the company doesn't know about. You are asking for consideration and the chance for discussion with those most qualified to give you counsel and make a decision. Good luck!

Advancement Within Field Selling

One of the great advantages of selling is that it permits, as does any specialized profession, advancement within itself. The successful salesman is considered an executive in his community. He represents the great names in American industry. He *is* his company in his franchised area. He is its aims, policies, ambitions. His conduct reflects his company's good name as well as his own. The stature of the salesman is growing in public opinion. Today's sales representative is an alert, solid thinking, community minded, up and coming young businessman.

Within itself, selling represents a challenging opportunity for the college graduate. The accomplished salesman has more control over his own destiny than do any of the others in business. Because self-development plays a larger role in selling than in other professions, there is constant opportunity for personal and financial growth. Many salesmen are looking elsewhere in their "status-seeking" attempts while status in great measure is right within their grasp. The opinion others have of you, your stature, your profession, your company, your community standing, your social standing, are what you make of them. They do not go automatically along with a title.

Many salesmen prefer to remain salesmen as do many family doctors who have no ambitions to become specialized. They are specialized enough. These salesmen practice the philosophy that it is better to be ten pounds overweight in the job they have than an ounce too light in the next one. Forward thinking managements applaud this attitude of salesmen who plan a lifetime career of selling. In fact, many companies are structuring their field sales activities to provide lifetime responsibility and financial growth, all within the field selling operations.

However, as mentioned earlier in this chapter, it is wise for you to plan for and prepare for the top sales assignments in your company and let destiny take its course. We said that only by aspiring for high goals can you attain any goal. The end result may well be a successful field sales career. This represents great accomplishment, not to be obtained without high goals and ambitions.

This book was written for the experienced, professional salesman. It is intended to help him enjoy the rich rewards which are well within his grasp. These rewards depend almost wholly upon his own self-development and ingenuity. The learning, growing process never stops for the salesman if he employs these new techniques now available to him for learning and making full use of the knowledge. The salesman who truly masters the arts and skills of ingenious selling will find both inner satisfaction and financial growth and security well within the sales profession.

Index

A

Account information as personal record of salesman, 83
Account lists, sources of, 91-92
Acquiring and employing good organizational habits, 65-79
  elements, 69-79
Acquiring fundamental skills for ingenious selling, 31-47
  awareness, definition of, 31
  six ways to develop awareness, 39-46
Advancement with company, do's and don't's for, 187-201
  plan, 192-199
  sales manager, responsibility of, 189-190
  within field selling, 200-201
Advantages of appointment with chain store buyer, 179
American Druggist, 43
American Management Association, 197
Analyzing buyer number one problem of salesman, 172-175
Angry buyer, 175-176
Applied experience as major element in good organization, 69-79
Appointment with chain store buyer:
  advantages, 179
  disadvantages, 179-180

B

Budgets responsibility of sales manager, 189
"Bumble bee" calls, 140
Business increase information as personal record of salesman, 84
Buyers, fourteen "type," 175-182
  all other "problem," 180-182
  angry, 175-176
  chain store, 179-180
  grudge, 175-176
  inscrutable, 177-178
  "new," 180-182
  "old friend," 180-182
  silent, 177-178
  small store, 180-181

Approaches, new, to solve major selling problems, 135-151
  big territory, controlling, 140-142
  buying committee, 142-147
  computer buying, 147-151
  working with supervisor, 136-140
Approaching selling situation, 155-157
Asset developed from liability, 17-23
Attitude as natural selling talent, 54-59
Awareness necessary for ingenious selling, 31-47

Record system (con't):
  business increase information, 84
  company records, 82-83
  outline of record form, 84-98
  territory information, 83-84
Role of questions in aiding idea creativity, 40
Routine of habit, avoidance of, 45-46

S

Sales manager, responsibilities of, 189-190
Sample job writeup, 75-76
Sample program for personal objectives projection, 67
Schedule, sample, for improvement of personal organization, 60-61
"Seeded" inventory system, 149
Selling, defined, 11-15
Selling material, too much, problem of, 184-186
Selling presentation, making, 159-161
Selling situation, approaching, 155-157
Seventeen sales problems and their solutions, 171-186
  all other "problem" buyers, 180-182
  analyzing buyer, 172-175
  angry buyer, 175-176
  chain store buyer, 179-180
  grudge buyer, 175-176
  inscrutable, 177-178
  "new" buyer, 180-182
  "old friend" buyer, 180-182
  price, 186
  silent buyer, 177-178
  small store buyer, 180-181
  successful buyer, 178-179
  talkative buyer, 178
  "too big" program, 182-184
  too much selling material, 184-186
  unsuccessful buyer, 178-179

Seventeen sales problems (con't):
  upset buyer, 175-176
  woman buyer, 176-177
Silent buyer, 177-178
Skills, fundamental, of ingenious selling acquired through everyday awareness, 31-47
  awareness, definition of, 31
  natural, of selling, 118-119
  six ways to develop awareness, 39-46
Small store buyer, 180-181
Sociability different from conversational ability, 104
Solving sales problems more effectively, 171-186
  all other "problem" buyers, 180-182
  analyzing buyer, 172-175
  angry buyer, 175-176
  chain store buyer, 179-180
  grudge buyer, 175-176
  inscrutable buyer, 177-178
  "new" buyer, 180-182
  "old friend" buyer, 180-182
  price, 186
  silent buyer, 177-178
  small store buyer, 180-181
  successful buyer, 178-179
  talkative buyer, 178
  "too big" program, 182-184
  too much selling material, 184-186
  unsuccessful buyer, 178-179
  upset buyer, 175-176
  woman buyer, 176-177
Sources of information in trade magazines, 43-44
Sources of wholesale lists, 91-92
Standard and Poor, 194
Successful buyer, 178-179
Supervisor, how to work with, 136-140

T

Talents for ingenious selling, inventory of, 49-64

Talents for ingenious selling (con't):
attitudes, 54-59
confidence, 50-54
personal organization, 59-64
Talkative buyer, 178
Territory, controlling large, 140-142
Territory information as personal record of salesman, 83-84
Territory structure, responsibility of sales manager for, 189
The Wall Street Journal, 121; 171; 195
Timing as natural selling skill, 118-119; 128-130
Toastmasters Club, 101
"Too big" program, problem of, 182-184
Too much selling material, problem of, 184-186
Trade magazines as sources of information, 43-44
Transfer from "considered" to "impulse" purchase, 8-11
Translating major selling problems into sales opportunities, 135-151
big territory, controlling, 140-142
buying committee, 142-147
computer buying, 147-151
working with supervisor, 136-140
Turning liability into asset, 17-23

U

"Umbrella selling," 182-184
Understanding people as natural selling skill, 119; 131-133
Unsuccessful buyer, 178-179

Upset buyer, 175-176
Using personal experiences to develop awareness, 44-45
Using record system for personal selling requirements, 81-98
account information, 83
business increase information, 84
company records, 82-83
outline of record form, 84-98
territory information, 83-84

V

Visual aids, use of, 184-186
Volume as responsibility of sales manager, 190

W

Wall Street Journal, 121; 171; 195
Ways, six, to develop awareness, 39-46
Ways, three, to improve confidence, 53-54
Weak interviews, how to turn into successful, 153-169
approaching selling situation, 155-157
following up on sale, 166-169
getting order, 161-166
introducing sale, 158-159
making selling presentation, 159-161
Wholesale lists, sources of, 91-92
Woman buyer, 176-177
Working with supervisor, 136-140
Workshop in Persuasive Communication, 100